THE
GRANTS GAME

THE
GRANTS GAME

by
Lawrence Lee

Published in San Francisco by
HARBOR PUBLISHING

Distributed by G.P. Putnam's Sons

Paperbound / ISBN 0-936602-03-1
Hardbound / ISBN 9-936602-18-3

For information contact Harbor Publishing,
1668 Lombard Street, San Francisco, California 94123

Jacket/Cover Illustration: Lynn Hollyn Associates
Jacket/Cover Printer: Alithochrome
Text Designer/Compositor: Abracadabra
Text Printer and Binder: Fairfield Graphics

to
Don and Jo and Louisa
for memories of the happy times
during the hunt

Table of Contents

Part Two: The Grants Handbook

Part Three: Appendixes

Introduction

Who am I, and why am I telling you all this?

A few years ago, some friends and I built a radio station with other people's money. I should say right away that this was a nonprofit radio station, since investors fight like animals to finance the other kind, the ones that can make money.

It took us about two years to raise the necessary quarter-million dollars. Admittedly, some of the money came from small public contributions—car washes, bake sales and individual subscription—but that only made the rest of our job easier. The bulk of the cash came from the most unlikely directions:

- From crusty old oil zillionaires, men who had bootstrapped themselves out of the oilfields and onto the decks of yachts and who, moreover, could be expected to suffer acute indigestion once they heard the radio station they were paying for, with its bright pink politics and its atonal music. (Dead, but equally crusty, zillionaires gave, too.)

- From big corporations, banks and refineries and the like, with no evident motive for diverting cash our way.

- From you and me, the taxpayer. Somehow, those checks were the best of all. (They're blue, with speckles all over them, and you can see the check itself right through the glassine window of its unstamped little envelope. For some reason, the first thing anyone does with one is smell it. They smell wonderful.)

In short, our modest project tapped every category of nonprofit support available. And what a smorgasbord of backing there was to choose from! Even in today's shaky market, which limits foundation revenues, and despite the era of limits produced by the taxpayers' revolt, the kind of support dispensed as grants stands somewhere above thirty billion dollars a year.

That's a remarkable figure. It says that individuals (and their estates), foundations, corporations and the government have joined to create and maintain an economic mechanism unique to our era, a money-machine that exists to finance the new, the creative, the necessary-but-unprofitable, the old-and-worth-keeping, the merely beautiful. The private gifts are a matter of private motives, but for most big business and all governments, this sort of philanthropy and support are given factors in their existence. We are far from the day when a Mozart or a Wagner had to risk his art upon the whims and fortunes of a petty royal, or when the poet had to complain of the "patron worse than a garret."

Begging with hat in hand has been replaced by the process that this book explains—grants, a way of nonprofit financing whose etiquette allows both sides, donor and recipient, to meet their own goals and to remain human in the bargain.

Whether you need a grant to complete a cycle of chamber music, to explore dark byways of the Prime Number Theory or to keep the child-care center running, the asking process is essentially the same. And although I'm almost certain that what you're trying to get money for is different from the radio station we built, I'm equally sure that the reasons you'll *get* the money are the same reasons we had. In fact, most of the reasons people win the grants game can be combined and reduced into a single rule so firm that I'm very tempted to call it a law:

YOU GET THE MONEY YOU NEED ONCE YOU UNDERSTAND WHY THEY'RE GOING TO GIVE IT TO YOU.

If you're into needlepoint, you could do worse than sew a sampler with that statement, meditating upon it as you work. It's the secret of this book, right here on page 3, putting you well ahead of people who always skip reading introductions.

And I've purposely given it the flavor of a zen *koan* because so many people who need help in getting grants ask for that kind of advice. As you'll learn, once you're successful with your own grants, word spreads and supplicants appear asking for the rule for, the knack of, even—God forbid—the *trick to* getting grants. You're like the hermit on the ledge in *The New Yorker* cartoons.

For several years now, warmhearted soul that I am, I've dispensed my hard-won advice to other radio and TV projects, to theater groups, community newspapers—even some Buddhists. (The Buddhists, by the way, were not of the zen stripe. They failed to digest and employ the rule quoted above, and their project flopped.)

So, to answer my own question, I'm somebody who has played the grants game and won, and I'm telling you all this so you can have the advice and counsel my friends and I got the hard way, by experience. I had been writing grant proposals for many months before I met somebody else with the same job, and I'd been at it a couple of years before I encountered my first team of professional fundraising counselors. At these first encounters we always had a crowded agenda, the nuts and bolts of our work. But afterward, over drinks or dinner, I soaked up their yarns about triumphs and failures and got an idea of the psychology and philosophy of nonprofit funding. What a comfort to know that every problem I'd run up against, somebody else had run up against—and, most often, had solved.

It's a feeling I want to share with you.

Who are you, and how can this book help you?

You're someone who needs money for something you believe in deeply. Maybe you're a painter or a biophysicist or a feminist paralegal—whoever you are, it's your project itself that's important, not the rigmarole involved in getting it funded. But, for now, you're ready to play the grants game so you can play the game you're really interested in.

As an individual or a part of a small organization, it's unlikely you'll ever have the services of a development (read: grant-writing) staff or department, and you want to learn the ropes without making an investment in time or money that might not pay off. You want proposals which can compete with those written by fundraising pros—and win. This book shows you how to create them.

The goal of this book is to help you play the grants game with that sense of effortlessness and rightness that champion athletes describe when they explain how it feels to win. You'll find, as you play, that the grants game is a continuous process, not a hit-and-run affair. It's a lot more like chess than capture-the-flag. You'll observe that the players who think of the game as "us against them," not "us *and* them," have set themselves up as losers, because the strategic secret of the grants game is to convince your funding sources that you and they are playing on the same team.

And I also predict that your successes with the grants game will make you more successful with your project itself, as my friends and I discovered. A grant application makes you sit down and think out your project in great detail—perhaps more detail than you've pondered before. The review and reporting often required by funding sources gives you a cue for reflection, and for making changes—a cue you might not give yourself. It will become difficult for you to enjoy a special triumph without sharing it with your funding source, or to meet with a prospective benefactor without at least laying the groundwork for one of the "shelter tokens" I talk about later in the book.

You're going to secure your first grant because of the momentum of the life and work experiences that have led you up to this point, but once you're comfortable with the grant process and have learned to budget time for the information-collecting and organizing chores described in Part Two of this book, the grant process really should feel like a game, a game you're comfortable with because you've won before and expect to win again.

To help you learn the game, this book is arranged in two distinct sections.

Part One is about the philosophy and psychology of getting grants. The section is designed, frankly, to help you overcome Fear of Fundraising and to approach the task armed with the experience of those who have gone before.

We'll begin by examining some folk wisdom—phrases and slogans that everyone who writes grant proposals eventually hears again and again. I believe deeply that a rough empiricism is at work here and that these proverbs have gained currency because each contains a truth worth considering. They also may help jiggle you out of some preconceptions, such as the idea that whatever you're raising money for is so special that only a handful of resources exist to support you.

And we'll visit the world of the people who make their living giving money away. As you'll learn, they're neither watchdogs nor misers-for-hire. Anxious matchmakers is a better description. I want to supply faces for the so-called faceless bureaucrats and lawyers many first-time grant applicants imagine as the judges of their labors.

We'll listen to the voices of the winners, men and women who have devised imaginative strategies for getting initial and continuing support for their projects. Again, their projects may differ from yours, but their tactics should translate into other fields—and they may suggest brand-new ones you can try.

This first part of the book is deliberately written in an informal, anecdotal style. It's a combination of reporting and my best advice on the frame of mind that successful grant writers appear to me to share. And it's a section you may want to turn to later, as you gather war stories to compare with those told in its pages. But, as I said, the basic idea is to offer you a caucus of friendly, motivating voices standing by to reassure you that you're not alone.

Part Two is a tool kit, a straightforward handbook to the grant-writing process. It's designed to be used over and over—in fact, every time you prepare a new proposal. Its headings allow you to skim the section, checking off each essential step in preparing a successful application.

We'll start by chopping up the job into several smaller jobs—a modular approach. (But don't worry, the modules are just file folders or manila envelopes. Whatever is handy.)

The first stage, prospect research, tells you how to widen your idea of where the money's going to come from. It contains specific procedures for discovering whether your needs match the giving goals of a prospective donor. (An Appendix, Prospect Research Resources, shows you how to track down grant targets in the first place.) After that we'll tackle the piece of writing at the heart of every successful grant, the case statement, a piece of prose you'll be using again and again.

A large part of every grant proposal is devoted to reassurance. Our next step is a crash-course in all the proposal elements that make a prospective donor feel good about sending you the money—the legal, bookkeeping/ accounting and tax questions, and the best ways to demonstrate the personal and institutional associations that show the proposal reader you're serious about what you're planning to do and capable of doing it.

Your relationship with the people who fund you doesn't end when you get the check, so there is a section of procedures for maintaining and nourishing the relationship, techniques that lay the groundwork for continuing support and for help in getting aid from fresh directions.

Nobody can provide you with an insurance policy against the bad breaks or scattered examples of bad faith I've seen dishearten even the most experienced and successful grant writers. But I can say with confidence that if you listen to the voices who speak in these pages, you'll be ahead of the game as you begin, and that you'll find it a game worth playing—and winning.

Sometimes when people familiar with the world of grants sit down to trade notes, they swap stories about the lucky break that came just in the nick of time. I side with the school that says we make our own luck. But I've also had some pleasant bolts from the blue. May you, as well.

Good luck.

Part One:

THE RULES
AND THE PLAYERS

Open Secrets

The grants game is such a big, complicated enterprise that different rules must apply to different circumstances. A government program, for example, may be obliged by law to adopt standards of pickiness, fairness or generosity that are strictly optional to the trustees of a private foundation. But since the grant process boils down to a tit-for-tat arrangement between giver and getter, rules emerge.

A lawyer of my acquaintance likes to say, "Free advice is worth exactly what you pay for it," and examples do spring to mind: John D. Rockefeller's famous "Buy low, sell high," or the advice of *Monopoly* inventor Charles Darrow to "get Boardwalk and Park Place and never go into debt." But when newcomers ask for help, veterans of the grants game give the same advice again and again. If the machinery of experience hasn't polished all of these aphorisms into gems worthy of *Bartlett's Familiar Quotations*, most of them at least exhibit the glint of semi-precious stones.

Let's start with my own grants game proverb (which really is just a succinct rephrasing of the most valuable piece of advice I ever got from a seasoned fundraiser):

You get the money you need once you understand why they're going to give it to you

I shouldn't spoil a good zen-style saying like that with close textual analysis, but I will, anyway, for the simple reason that many—all too many—grants game beginners go into the fray with a chip on their shoulder. Their attitude is essentially this: The prospective donor is awash in what they need so desperately: namely, money. Taxpayer money, confiscated by legislators. Ill-gotten gains superintended by some robber baron's foundation. Corporate money, doled out a bit at a time to soothe consciences troubled by easy victories in the netherworld of commerce.

To some extent, of course, they're right. As a President once told us, life isn't fair, and while every Utopia, from Thomas More's original right down to today's complex theories of distributive justice, tries to puzzle out a way to legislate fairness, the project remains pending. We're stuck with one of those realities of contemporary life, and those of us who need the money have to make peace with ourselves about the ones who parcel it out.

Two bad attitudes sometimes assert themselves after prolonged meditation on your needs versus their riches.

The first is to take the money and ignore the spirit in which it was given . . . grab it and run. This is the case in which the grant recipient boasts that his blank-verse epic on the evils of the oil industry was written during a sabbatical funded by the refining subdivision of Synergistic Interglom Corporation. An extreme instance was the young Nelson Rockefeller's support of the Mexican painter Diego Rivera. Placed in charge of the decoration of Rockefeller Center in the 1930s, the young tycoon hired the brilliant and progressive artist to paint murals in the lobby. Rivera's mural included a vignette of vampire-like financiers in evening clothes. One bore more than a passing resemblance to John D. Rockefeller, Mr. Buy-Low-Sell-High himself. The younger Rockefeller wound up having the mural painted over. After the whole affair was finished, both sides stood exactly where they had at the beginning. Rivera's moral victory was confined to occasional obscure references, like this one, and Rockefeller went on to become even richer than he started and, doubtless, wary of dealing with living artists who didn't share his politics.

The other bad attitude, of course, is tugging the forelock and selling out. A toady Diego Rivera, for example, would have portrayed John D. with bulging, new-socialist-realism biceps, leading the masses toward freedom and plenty.

The truth is, the real conflicts of the grants game are as far as possible from these extreme cases—they're in the center, in the arena of overlapping motives and of compromise.

Luckily, the task of administering all the nonprofit billions expended these days has become so big and complicated that it's in the hands of specialists. They're the mediators between the motives of the big givers they work for and the desires of the applicants whose proposals are stacked on their desks. Together, these people form a new segment of society we might dub the philanthropic class. F. Scott Fitzgerald was right when he noted that the very rich are different from you and me, but the members of the philanthropic class are a bit less different, and it's a difference that counts.

Example. Hardly a community in America has been left untouched by the generosity of the Ford Foundation. Schools, hospitals, museums, works of art and music and literature, innovation in law, theater, public broadcasting—all have flowed from the profits generated by the residue of Henry Ford's personal fortune. In person and in his lifetime, Henry Ford was reputed to be a thoroughgoing bigot. Yet, for millions of Americans, the Ford Foundation is what comes to mind when we hear the word "foundation," and the intelligence and thoughtfulness with which the Ford grants are administered inspire many smaller givers.

The Ford Foundation's motive isn't to clean up Henry Ford's smudged image, nor is it to sell cars; the Motor Company is quite separate. The professionals at America's Number One Foundation are giving money to applicants whose projects will contribute to that foundation's goals. Despite their board members, most foundations, Ford included, really are run by the staff, the people who work there nine-to-five, five days a week. They, not some dead tycoon, are writing the checks. And, of course, they, not the founder, are reading your grant proposal. The smart grant writer will sit down and analyze Ford's giving pattern, discovering early in the game that Ford likes to start things, not save things in trouble. Thus, it would be exactly the wrong place to turn with a worthy project failing for lack of local support. Ford likes to support a diversity of innovative projects, not gain a name in a narrow area of specialization, as Andrew Carnegie did with his nationwide string of free public libraries. Therefore, it might not be wise to hit the Ford Foundation with a proposal that carbon-copies a project you know they funded in a city a thousand miles away. (But that technique works like magic with foundations that do one, or a few, things well—again and again.)

I'm not trying to instruct you in the fine points of applying to the Ford Foundation, but to help you see that a philosophy of giving is at work in funding institutions. It is usually changing all the time, in response to available funds or new legislation or a lively feedback from earlier beneficiaries, who report which projects are clicking and which are not worth supporting further. But this philosophy, however informal, is the product of the same living, breathing men and women you'll be dealing with as a grants game player.

The secret is to discover and understand the goals that the people giving the money away believe they are trying to meet. The easy way to discover these goals is simply to ask. Most funding programs supply the underwriting legislation or the annual report as a matter of course to applicants wise enough to ask, and learning the giver's goals should be your primary job in any personal or telephone contact with the proposal readers. (There are, of course, motives for giving which the members of the philanthropic class are unlikely to confess—at least in your early conversations. More accurately put, they're motives for *not* giving, and fear is in first place.)

Government grant administrators work, technically, for you and me, the voters. Actually, of course, they work for tenured bureaucrats who are likely to remain with the agency after the program the grant team oversees has lost its funding. And they work for Congress and the committee specialists there who write the bills that pay the bills. Thus, while government grant administrators are usually looking for projects that closely match the guidelines in the law that created the program, they're also looking for grants that won't land them in hot water. Lately, with economic troubles, the heat has been severe. *Harper's* magazine recently printed a frontal attack on the National Endowment for the Humanities, arguing essentially that that government is best which supports the humanities least. British novelist Kingsley Amis got space in *The New York Times* to assault government support of music, pointing out that the great classical composers had no help from the National Endowment for the Arts. (Amis conveniently ignored help they had from their royal or wealthy patrons.) And Senator William Proxmire has made a monthly ritual (and a rather dull book) out of his Golden Fleece Award. These "prizes" mock grants in pure science which appear to him to have no practical application, and they betray an ignorance of the step-at-a-time approach real science must take. Gadflies like these represent a general trend in the society, and the wise grant administrator devotes some worry to it. So does the wise grant applicant.

So, my advice that you'll get the money you need once you understand why they're going to give it to you simply means that giving doesn't happen in a vacuum. It happens because your project matches very closely the motives of the people who will help you.

Final example. In the mid-1970s, I worked with an experimental television newscast which had received more than $15 million from the Ford Foundation. True to the policy I mentioned earlier—Ford's desire to start things and send them into the world on their own—the Foundation announced it was cutting us loose. Their message was that our city itself had to love our experimental newscast, or lose it.

Our fundraisers went to work. Television news in those days cost a minimum $2 million a year. Our newscast was local, so we needed a local giver who, in turn, needed for some reason to give money away on that scale, locally. The giver was there. Across town at the headquarters of the biggest bank in the world, the people in charge of that bank's nonprofit grant program were looking for a way to eliminate, or tone down, their bank's image of hugeness and remoteness. Paying for our news show was exactly the ticket. Wisely or not, station management rejected the bank's money, and the show went off the air, but the point was that the grant specialists had done their job perfectly. They understood why the bank wanted to give them the money, and they very nearly cashed in.

The people who give money away are looking for partners in their enterprise—grant recipients whose work, while independent, is going to enhance the funding body's self-esteem and reputation. They are not like Michael Anthony, for many years personal secretary to the mysterious John

Beresford Tipton, sent into the world with cashier's checks. Old Tipton got his jollies when the million dollars came back at the end of each episode of *The Millionaire.* The real-life Tiptons are often dead, distant or never see the money, as money. The real-life Michael Anthonys want the money to stay where they sent it and to go to work, producing results that make them and their organization feel better about themselves.

To understand why they're going to give you the money, you'll have to be a bit of a psychologist and a bit of a detective. You'll have to use some of the magic that actors and novelists use when they climb inside someone else's head. What the givers say and write about themselves is your starting point, and you can get good clues from applicants who have dealt with those givers before.

Be relentless, like Spade or Marlowe, and don't waste your time mailing in the proposal until the giver's goals are crystal-clear to you. Try to know them so well that the administrator will finish reading your proposal and say, "I feel as though I wrote that myself."

Offer them the biggest bang for the buck

Everyone agrees that money is power, but the people reading your grant proposal are money pros, men and women acutely aware that the power of the money they give away varies greatly from applicant to applicant, from project to project.

I winced the first time I heard a professional grant expert use the phrase "biggest bang for the buck," but he was wearing a $600 suit and deserved his ranking at the top of his profession. He trotted out the phrase (which I assume originated somewhere in advertising) to shock me out of my wet-behind-the-ears attitude that altruism reigns supreme in the world of non-profit funding.

He was right, it doesn't.

The people who write the checks at foundations, in the government and at big businesses are full-time money pros who are working both sides of the ledger, income and expense. I've never met one who believed his or her program had—or ever would have—enough cash to satisfy the pageant of need and desire represented by the grant proposals accumulating in the in-basket. The limits they sense are real.

Take government. Staff members at the National Institutes of Health or the Endowments for the Arts and the Humanities believe themselves to be choosing *from among* worthy recipients. (There's no thought of sending a bit less to everyone who qualifies.) Politicians sense that the public resents impoundment of its earnings as taxes to be dispensed by bureaucrats. As a result, the bureaucrats are searching relentlessly for the projects that will justify the program's survival to both critics and public. They're looking for the biggest bang for the tax buck.

Take foundations. The people who read your proposal and send you the check are (or work alongside) the same people responsible for nursing the endowment that is generating the income. Foundations are conservative. They don't, as a rule, invest in alleged hedges like porcelain plates and uncut diamonds. Neither, of course, do they dip into their capital, the principal of the endowment; that's a sin ranking right up there with incest and patricide. Thus, when the market is shaky, as it has been for quite a while now, the emotion the money managers feel is basic and logical. It's fear—fear that with less money to give away, the foundation may need fewer people around to do the job. Their every goal is to do as much, or more, with dwindling resources as they did back in the days when their investments thrived. They're looking for the biggest bang for the foundation buck.

Take corporations. Wherever charitable grants appear in a company's ledgers, they're really part of advertising and public relations. You'll search far and wide for a business that writes philanthropy into its articles of incorporation. (The shareholders, or the owning family, would have management's head on a platter the minute it was proposed.) But many, if not yet most, companies of a certain size have realized, like the bank I told you about, that good deeds are good business. Somewhere in the organization are a group of people who want to keep their jobs (or a vice president who wants to maintain the program as a matter of personal prestige or office politics), arguing that the company is morally obliged to keep giving money away. Across the conference table from them is the vice president in charge of advertising. He's saying that, with profits down, the company had better spend that money advertising their product. Otherwise, there won't be money to pay their salaries, much less give away. Obviously, businesses that make grants are looking for the same thing they seek in their advertising: the biggest bang for the buck.

Naturally, the survival of the grant program you're applying to won't hinge on your handiwork. But it's an entirely safe assumption that your proposal competes with others that match the ground-rules. The winners are the proposals that make the money managers believe they'll deliver the maximum results with the minimum risk.

Whether the grant readers work in the public sector or the private, they're gauging your proposal by the same standards of efficiency and cost-effectiveness that prevail within their own organization and, in a larger sense, within our society, which places a premium on the benefits of competition.

Those of us who apply for grants often are those least familiar with this brand of hard-nosed analysis. As writers, artists, scientists or professionals accustomed to working alone or in small, teamwork settings, we recoil at the coldness of it all. If we're lucky enough—if lucky is the word—to have some experience of budget-making (and trimming) in a large organization, so much the better.

Ask yourself whether, for example, you can do what you propose more cheaply than your competitor? That is, if you're asking for a grant to study the physics of wave action, could you do the job in nearby Lake Erie? If your competitor proposes fieldwork in the south of France and includes a budget line for a research assistant of the opposite sex, you may—as the letters from *Reader's Digest* Sweepstakes always say—already have won.

Ask yourself whether the professional biography in your proposal tells the reader that the project at hand is the next logical step in a career of demonstrated promise and achievement. If so, you're ahead of the game again.

Remember, the game isn't roulette, and it isn't letters to Santa Claus. It's a transaction: something you need in exchange for something they need. Usually it amounts to the money you need in exchange for the enhancement of their prestige as money managers.

Not only should your grant proposal convince your readers that your project matches the guidelines of their program, it should suggest that you'll do the job better than anybody else possibly could with the same money, and that they'll be proud they chose you.

Don't put all your eggs in one basket

Not even imaginary eggs—all those zeroes on that check you're hoping for.

A lot of first-time grants game players get started because a colleague or a professional bulletin tells them about a grant program that appears tailor-made to support their endeavor. They hurl themselves into writing the proposal, mail it off and endure weeks or months of silence until, among the bills one morning, they receive a courtesy note listing the people who won out. The grant proposal gets tossed out in the next cleanup, and the applicant becomes an embittered veteran of the grants game, somebody who never wants to play again.

The smart player wouldn't dream of applying to only one place. Writing the proposal is too much work to be expended in a single shot and, whether you realize it yet or not, there are too many attractive targets for your labors to go to waste in this fashion.

Professional fundraisers and grant writers spend the bulk of their time in an exercise called prospect research. They're making their own good luck by multiplying the number of bets they can place with the same chip, their grant proposal. They know that many foundations share similar fundraising goals, as do corporations, and that government programs—even those for facilities or grants in pure research—often are duplicated or supplemented by similar programs on the state or municipal level. Later in the book, I'll show you, step-by-step, how to conduct prospect research on your own, but the point here is that you should consider it essential. If you're reading this book because you're racing a deadline for a specific grant program, read on and meet the deadline, but keep in mind that the one-shot application is bush league tactics in the grants game.

Why? Let me offer another proverb: *money loves company*.

The money managers who oversee grant programs generally dislike intensely the idea of supporting anything that relies entirely upon their largesse. They're on the lookout for proposals that suggest momentum, progress, the continuation of work begun under other auspices (even if strictly your own) and continuing with help from them—among others.

The people who give money away prefer to supply the minimum amount necessary for you to complete your budget and go to work, but if they sense you're asking them for the whole kit and kaboodle, down to the last postage stamp, they're likely to turn their attention to some other applicant who appears to have made more progress without their aid and, in general, strikes them as more realistic and self-reliant.

If you're seeking a federal grant, the managers want to know what success you've had from local sources—the city, the state, your sheltering institution. If you're involved in a community resource project, how much support has your community itself supplied? Other nonprofit institutions you're involved with?

The budget pages of your proposal will make this clear, and they should paint a picture of teamwork and collaboration.

If your project is relatively big and complicated, but exists strictly on paper, or in your head, how in the world do you go about satisfying this requirement? The answer is to imagine, and then make real, a system of support in which each source of help relies upon the goodwill and, eventually, the actual cash support of all the others.

Let me explain how my friends and I built that radio station, and as I do, try to translate our situation into yours and see if the tactics are useful in your own case. We learned, early on, that the Department of Education (or HEW, as it was then) made money available to build new, nonprofit radio stations. Not all the money we needed, mind you, but a significant part of our total budget. They wanted assurances that individual contributors, large and small, would join them in this enterprise, and that the FCC would permit us to go on the air. The FCC, meanwhile, didn't care to give us a license until it was convinced that the Department of Education and all of our individual contributors were serious. And, needless to say, our individual contributors—especially the large donors and the foundations—were extremely reluctant to part with cash if both of the government agencies weren't in the bag.

What an impasse.

We solved it by having everybody involved explain to each other, in writing wherever possible, what they were prepared to do if our plan crystallized.

The millionaires and the foundations said, in letters that bore the weight of contract, they would ante up if everybody else did. They, the FCC and the Department of Education were impressed by several thousand cards from individuals in our town who said, in effect, "The day the FCC gives its go-ahead, bill me for a membership in your public radio station."

It worked. The Department of Education came through first, knowing it wouldn't have to give us the money unless the FCC agreed. In a series of unusual (but legally kosher) meetings with bemused members of the FCC, we invited them to telephone contributors, large and small, at random and at our expense, to assure themselves that the pledges demonstrated in our application were real. With the FCC's approval, our local foundations and corporations and individual contributors chipped in, bills went out to subscribers and the station went on the air.

This was teamwork on a big scale. Subscribers didn't want to send money to an imaginary radio station. The FCC didn't want to issue a license to an imaginary radio station, and the Department of Education *couldn't*, by law, fund an imaginary radio station. The radio station came true because everybody involved wound up believing in each other as much as they believed in us, the people who thought it up.

Don't let the fact that your project isn't a noncommercial FM station blind you to the principle at work here. Every grant proposal should, to the greatest degree possible, demonstrate this same spirit of collaboration.

Imagine that you're seeking a grant to pursue pure research in a relatively narrow area of science. It may look like a lonely transaction between you and your funding target, but it probably isn't. For example, if the grant comes through, would the school or agency you work for release you from certain teaching or staff duties to pursue the work? Have your boss say so in writing, estimate the value of the time involved, and demonstrate as a gift-in-kind in both the budget and shelter sections of your proposal.

Imagine that you're applying for grants to maintain a day-care center. How much support can you show from fees charged to parents who use it? From CETA workers supplied by the city program? The difference between the rent you pay and what the landlord would charge to a *for*-profit enterprise?

Grants game pros know that the money they need converges upon their projects from many directions. It doesn't drop out of the blue in one large, green hunk. A look at the budget of most successful nonprofit enterprises of a certain size shows that a great deal of the money, perhaps as much as half, comes from a relative handful of large contributors, such as wealthy people, foundations, corporations or the government. Another quarter may come from fifty to a hundred well-to-do individuals, or from token or "consolation" grants from local companies and foundations whose pattern is to make many small gifts. The rest could represent money from the people who use the enterprise (such as child-care fees) or the booked, in-kind value of gifts from the people working on the project, such as an accounting of unpaid (and forgiven, meaning forgotten) salary.

If your project is relatively big and complex, there's another lesson to learn about the way money managers think. To you and me, money may be money, but to them it splits into two distinct categories: capital and operations. Capital means the money you spend to rent the space, buy or lease the equipment, get insurance and so on—the money it takes to get a roof over things and get started. Operations money is what you spend for salaries, materials that get used up, telephones and other services.

Some government programs and many foundations limit their help to one-time-only grants of seed money to cover capital costs. They're telling you, in effect, "We believe in what you're setting out to do, and here's some money to get started—but don't keep hitting us up for help." Others feel just the opposite way. They're willing to assess the momentum and success of a project that's already underway and then to share with others the job of supplying the minimum amount necessary to keep the ball rolling.

But the key word here is *share.*

When your grant application shows in black and white how many other people and institutions already believe in your project, the likelier you are to win a new believer and get the grant you need.

Charity begins at home

Thanks to America's appetite for beef and gasoline, the town where I grew up in the Southwest was positively packed with millionaires. Cadillacs swarmed the freeways, and a shopping trip meant Neiman-Marcus, not K-Mart.

Among these millionaires was one I'll call Waldo C. Buckner. As it turned out, he wasn't the richest man in town; it only looked that way. That's because the local college played football in the Waldo C. Buckner Stadium, planes landed at the Waldo C. Buckner International Airport and culture reposed in the Waldo C. Buckner Museum. A lot of people get things named after them once they're dead, but Waldo C. Buckner liked to see his name chiseled in granite while he was still alive. For him, charity not only began at home, it ended there.

Unless you live in a remote corner of Saskatchewan, it's likely that your very own Waldo C. Buckner, or his estate, is waiting for your grant application. Rich people and the foundations they leave behind have a practical and sentimental interest in spending their money at home and so, to an even greater extent, do corporations, who consider it good business to look better in the eyes of their neighbors.

Grants game novices often envision the distant targets of their proposals as akin to Glinda, the Good Witch of the North, arriving in a green bubble to wave her wand and grant wishes the home town folks would never understand. But, just as in *The Wizard of Oz*, the folks with the wands are interested in seeing what you can do for yourself without their help. Home is exactly the place to start, and "home" can mean your state or province or region, if not your home town itself. As you'll see later in the book, a rich variety of small foundations exists and you can find them easily thanks to the good offices of a foundation that specializes in helping applicants and donors get together—the Foundation Center and its indispensable Foundation Directory.

But the other important reason to start at home is to have a practice field for the over-all strategy that all grants game winners share.

Human contact.

Meetings, telephone calls, negotiations, lunch—everything possible that puts you in direct and interactive touch with the people who are going to give you the money.

Grants game losers get stuck in the letters-to-Santa psychology that puts undue emphasis on the written proposal. They type it up, mail it off, cross their fingers and wonder why they get passed over.

The winners all have burned into their brains the most important grants game proverb of them all . . .

People give money to people

Do you remember the story of Dumbo, the flying elephant?

As you'll recall, Dumbo was as aerodynamically unstable as your next baby elephant, but the gigantic ears that made him a figure of fun around the circus were the secret of his ability to fly. Nevertheless, because he really didn't believe in himself, he put his faith in a magic feather he clutched tightly in his trunk upon takeoff. Eventually, of course, he lost the feather just at the moment it was essential to fly—and he flew anyway.

Your written grant proposal is Dumbo's feather. You can fly without it. It's only a token.

Too many grants game beginners concentrate on the proposal—which is, after all, only part of the playing equipment—and thus wind up losing sight of the game itself. Wide margins, neat typing, lucid prose, early postmark, spiffy binding. They can *help*, sure. But they're not the heart of the game.

The grants game is a confidence game in the best sense of that phrase. You'll get the money you need when the people from whom you're asking it come to share *your* confidence in yourself and in your project. "People give money to people" is such an important (and familiar) rule in the world of nonprofit funding that it's what I wanted to call this book. (My editor dissuaded me by pointing out how much it sounds like one of those awful oil company advertising slogans.)

The money management pros at the foundations, corporations and government agencies are looking not only at the bare-bones summary of your project that the written proposal represents, they're looking at *you*. If they have trouble seeing you, they may begin to suspect that you're hiding behind the prose in your proposal—perhaps prose confected by a freelance grant writer, prose you may not live up to.

Anybody who ever got burned on a blind date knows how many appealing, even accurate, little facts a well-meaning matchmaker can string together to make a frog sound like a prince or a princess. That's what the money managers are afraid of as they read proposals from people they don't know. The grants game isn't a blind date—or even computer dating. It's more like old-fashioned courtship with its introductions and chaperones.

Many grants game beginners make the mistake of treating the written proposal as a great equalizer, a way of making competing applicants reduce their arguments to more or less identical form so the weighing of merits can proceed in a benign vacuum. This is the way courts of law work—or are supposed to. It's not the way the grants game works.

Just like bankers pondering a loan or business people considering a limited partnership, the money managers of the grants world consider themselves involved in judgments about people. The paperwork is simply a tool, a memory-aid.

Their job is to judge you without wasting time and energy, and your job is to overcome their fear of the unknown without making a bloody nuisance of yourself, to establish yourself as the thinking, planning, competent human being you know you are. If you don't do this, someone the givers know better will beat you out for the money.

Fortunately, the givers arrange their working lives so that they can meet applicants. This is why you'll find them at professional meetings and conventions, at arts festivals, at openings and at more-or-less formal seminars and lunches. The funding groups with nationwide applicants send representatives around the country or rely on local stand-ins who help make these judgments.

For these reasons, there's almost nothing more helpful to your effort than time well spent with these money managers (and almost nothing more devastating than making a poor first impression).

If you're applying to a funding body across the country, you may have to make do with telephone contacts in which you find your way through whatever bureaucracy's involved to the person who'll be the main reader of your proposal. (And if your project is big enough, the application important enough, you may want to visit them anyway, or send a stand-in of your own.)

But if you're concentrating on the local level, as I've insisted that you should, a letters-only relationship with your targets is not only stupid, it's probably fatal to your enterprise. If funding professionals receive a possibly worthy proposal from utter strangers, they may initiate the contact on their own, but your tactic must be to beat them to it.

How? Use every chance you can to make in-person contact. Don't ask for background material and application forms on their programs to be mailed if you can go by the office to pick them up. Don't pick up the material from the receptionist and leave if you can have a word with one of the people who will be reading the finished application. (And don't discount the importance of the receptionist or a junior staff member if that's as far as you can get.)

If you manage to combine a brief conversation with one of these routine errands, be prepared to ask intelligent and pertinent questions and to state your case if given the chance. Don't overstay your welcome, don't spend any time whatsoever knocking the competition and don't come on like a know-it-all. When the time comes to hand in the grant proposal, try to do that in person, too.

This personal foot-in-the-door strategy I've described is a worst-case situation. By far the best method of meeting the givers is through mutual friends or acquaintances.

Every source of money is surrounded by a network of interested outsiders. In the world of government grants, for example, these outsiders might be regional specialists or national committees of review, drawn from within the discipline. Critics and curators and chairmen of departments are demigods to certain large foundations and to the National Endowments for the Arts and the Humanities. Corporations listen to the opinion of their boards of directors and their advertising and public relations agencies.

These networks can be especially busy, and important, around local foundations, corporations and grant-making individuals. Just as you must plumb the motives of the money managers you're dealing with, you'll need to find out what makes these middlemen (and women) tick. Some typical networkers I've observed around local foundations in big-city settings include:

- *The lawyer.* Paid for his advice on business matters, he offers it free in the context of charity. For some reason, lawyers feel even more keenly about the free advice they give than the kind that's bought and paid for. His main motive is to come up with projects that'll increase his standing in the eyes of the client. His payoff from you is shared pride in the success of your project, but he may be likelier than other helpers to demand a role in making decisions about the direction of that project. Your goal in handling him is to make him *feel* indispensable without letting him *become* indispensable.

- *The minister.* (Priest or rabbi.) Some of the worldliest advice I've ever received on fundraising has come from men wearing clerical collars. For certain givers, the cleric's imprimatur is essential.

- *The hostess.* She may be the widow of the fortune's founder or a woman of independent means who fills her time by doing good works. Good works may take the form of delightful dinners served by her domestic staff and remain good works nonetheless. Her payoff may lie more in the social ritual than in her standing among her peers, and your job is to be the perfect guest (which means being grateful and attentive during the long stretch between dinners). Becoming the extra man (or woman) on her guest list can be worth a 500-foot stack of brilliantly-written proposals.

- *The black sheep.* He inherited part of the fortune, but they won't let him near the business. (He may have gotten in trouble in college, back in the 40s. There may have been a drinking problem.) His goal: bring in projects that make him look better in the eyes of his doubting relatives.

Every seasoned fundraiser knows these types, and more. The world of grants is as richly and diversely populated as a Dickens novel, and the surprise turns of plot can be just as intricate. The successful player navigates this world with a variety of comfortable social strategies—and the key word in that phrase is *comfortable.*

Many who apply for nonprofit grants are accustomed to working alone or in small groups. There's nothing antisocial about this. It's simply that, today, invisible barriers exist between many specialized worlds of work and art and the world at large. Sometimes our projects are difficult or impossible to explain to lay persons. Going into the world at large to fetch back money can involve dressing up for dinner with rich strangers, listening to well-meaning but incorrect recitals of your work and the general strain of repeated social encounters in which your goal is to get some of what they have.

Realizing that you have something they want is half the battle, but for many fund-raisers the other half is in their heads. They find the "people" aspect of fund-raising painful or impossible.

All of the grants game winners are operating within a psychological framework that tells them there's nothing essentially demeaning about the game itself. Some winners would never dream things were otherwise, but others have to adopt personal analyses of the grant process to make them feel better about it. For example, I feel okay about the games metaphor that runs through this book and my conversations on the subject. Perhaps it's a metaphor that only a croquet player could understand, but I find the grants game precisely as civilized (and competitive, and bloodthirsty) as a cutthroat game of croquet. I like both games.

To win, you'll have to think up your own way of relating to the world of grants, of devising a public, fundraising face that's at home with whoever you are behind the scenes. For many of us, this seems literally two-faced—an abandonment of the wholeness and authenticity which modern life (and certainly modern therapies) value so highly.

In a recent book called *The Fall of Public Man*, social psychologist Richard Sennett recalls the day, about 300 years ago, when public life was livelier—a humming clockwork, a genuine marketplace of ideas. People back then could choose personalities depending upon which was more useful—the public one (mask-like, ritualized and often terribly effective) or the private one (much like today's valued authentic, whole person). It was like changing out of blue jeans to go to dinner. Today, with Vanderbilts wearing blue jeans, it isn't so easy to figure out who to be and when.

But the people Sennett wrote about had figured out ways to use each other without hurting each other, a valuable quality in social forms, and forms like these still thrive in the world of grants.

Take your own sponsoring committee or board of directors. ("Please," I heard somebody say.) What are their roles? They trade the clout they bring to the board for clout the board parcels out to them—a say in whatever is going on. Everybody who raises money has a board of directors, whether it's called for by the articles of incorporation and actually meets and takes minutes, or not. If you're in a solo line of work, your "board" consists of the colleagues, mentors and interested outsiders who lend their names, through direct contact and endorsements, to your proposal.

Critics of modern corporate life make much of the interlocking directorates among major companies, but that's a reason for boards of directors, and it's certainly a useful tactic to adopt for the grants game.

Whenever I've had to put together a board or a sponsoring committee for fund-raising, one goal has been to secure as many directors as possible who also sit as directors of groups that give money away. But all of the types I mentioned before in connection with foundations can come in handy—the lawyer, the minister, the hostess, the rich black sheep. A banker might help you bank and a realtor could keep your rent down, if your enterprise requires that kind of help. And the small-businessman can be indispensable, because he can talk sense about the realities of budget-making, the big difference between bookkeeping and accounting and when to pay bills, (a month or two late, as the big corporations do.) But the board member's real utility comes in two rituals of the world of grants.

First is prospect research, the medium-to-large sized meeting in which you and your board (or off-board advocates) figure out how much each prospective source of money is likely to grant.

Second is the solicitation itself, which is described in detail in the second part of this book. It involves double-teaming (usually by you or another "staff" pro and one board member, closest to the target) a single representative of the group you want money from. Government bodies and very large corporations have immunized themselves against this tactic, but it's so successful that it really deserves its status as ritual on the local fund-raising scene.

You may be lucky enough to find advocates, mentors or sponsors who revel in the process. When direct solicitation is unnecessary or impossible, their contribution comes through informal contacts which reinforce very forceful and formal written statements of their backing. Players like these love the game, sometimes as much or more than the particular team they're playing on at the time. When you get them on your team, pamper them like the stars they are.

Your advocates and allies are your most powerful tools in informally getting across the key points that will make your proposal attractive to the people who give money away. These points are:

- Your proposal has been written with the giver's goals and needs about the transaction in mind.

- You acknowledge the competitiveness of the situation and have planned carefully to make your project the best possible use of the money.

- You're realistic about the diverse sources of funding most projects require and have packed the financial pages of your proposal with proof of such diverse support for your project, starting at home.

- Finally and most important, your project is endorsed, supported, directly advised or materially aided by men and women with solid reputations for good sense and follow-through, people who make the money you're about to receive an excellent nonprofit investment.

Let's meet some of the players.

Givers and Takers

Now that I've sketched in for you what I consider the basic rules of the grants game, you can go directly to the Handbook that lies ahead and begin work on your own grant system. But in case you have a spare half-hour now, or can find one later, I have some stories I would like to tell you about the way the grants game *feels*. And not just the way it feels to the people playing to get the money. I want to talk about the people who give it away, too, because, for the intelligent grant-getter, these people hold—or should hold—the utmost fascination.

I promised at the beginning that I would try to give you a sense of the emotional tone of this complicated game, and my motive is the good-manager's motive I mentioned before: prevention of surprise. Some first-time grant-seekers are surprised by the breadth of their hope, the depth of their despair and the sheer, old-fashioned hatred that the grant process inspires in them. Passionate hope is okay, and so is fear translated into useful caution, but the hatred usually isn't justified. More times than not, it occurs as the result of mistaking a person—the grant officer—for the institution, the enabling statute, or the constricting rules he or she is obliged to follow in deciding against you. A friendly critic of mine has said that some of the stories I'm about to tell you strike her as almost maudlin—a violin solo for the givers. While a touch of pathos is useful in humanizing those who are distant ciphers, I don't want you weeping over them or believing that they are a tribe of Pickwicks and Pollyannas, uniformly well-meaning and nice to know. Nor, later on, when I introduce you to a couple of takers who play the game as genial sharpies, am I suggesting that sheer cunning is standard equipment for the successful grants game player.

Rather, I shall be trooping these players before you in an effort to convey a few concrete glimpses of one fundraiser's personal experiences in the field. If the emotions don't translate easily, perhaps the general lessons will.

But first I want to discuss the most important general lesson about the players and the forces that govern them—a lesson that by definition is the very hardest for a newcomer to grasp: a sense of the way things are at any given time in the world of nonprofit funding. Perhaps a good metaphor is the way the tide runs—a matter not only of tidal forces, but of local currents that may provide interesting backwashes against the prevailing trend. The important point is not merely to seek out an accurate reading on the way things stand on the day you set out to raise money, but to try to figure out how things got that way in the first place and how they will change next.

As this was written, in the early months of a Republican administration elected on a platform of trimming fat from government spending, a variety of programs—from employment development through arts support to the hardest of hard science—had been led to the block, and the drumbeats were continuing. Entire multi-billion-dollar programs threatened to vanish from the reference listings at the back of this and similar books, with only the distant whimpering of their clients and administrators to mark their passing. In other cases, the cries of pain and outrage perhaps were sufficient to identify the programs which could not be cut, and which were saved only because the political risk of making the cuts appeared to outweigh the political gain. Understanding the forces at work in a situation like this should, ideally, give you a sense of how to utilize the situation and possibly even change it. I'll begin, then, with some stories of players on both teams of the grants game—men and women who realize how important it is to remember that . . .

Things change

Philanthropy is thriving. Philanthropy is dying. They're giving away more money than ever before. The money they're giving away was never worth less. The taxpayers won't stand it any longer. The taxpayers want only things that really work.

If you listen long enough, you can hear it any way you want it, and even apparently contradictory statements sometimes both manage to be true. The one common thread in the world of grants is that the whole picture is always *changing*, and changing in ways that themselves change.

Back, for a moment, to the example of the first days of the new Republican administration in 1981. The proposed cuts in arts funding met spirited opposition very early on. When the President telephoned a Los Angeles drama critic to plug an old friend's failing play, the critic ragged Reagan unmercifully about the cuts, telling him he should be ashamed of himself and, after confirming with the White House that it had indeed been the President on the line, printed the whole embarrassing exchange. Less than two days after Ronald Reagan was wounded by a would-be assassin, Johnny Carson described the funding cuts on nationwide television as "the worst thing to happen to the arts since Ronald Reagan signed with Warner Brothers."

By the time you read this, the fate of Reagan's proposed cuts should be a matter of record and you, as something of an expert on grants, should know what that fate was. Consider: Did the Republican administration make all the cuts it wanted? Did many, or even any, of the beneficiary groups face extinction, as some of their (Hollywood) star witnesses assured Congress would happen?

Probably not. The first reaction to the proposed cuts was the creation of an arts coalition composed of groups which, only months earlier, hardly spoke to one another, so keen was their competition for a supposedly larger body of funding. More pointed and direct appeals were made by public fine arts charities for corporate and individual support, naming the cuts as a threat, and according to some early reports were being answered. Oddly, it appears that some organizations may have found themselves with a delightful spurt of income as money continued in the twilight of the older, more generous programs and would-be saviors appeared from fresh directions.

For fundraisers who take the long view, neither this nor several other possible scenarios should be surprising. The handwriting about government cutbacks was on the wall long before the proposed fact. Even the most theoretical and principled national politics trail, by months and years, signals that politicians make it their profession to read and that canny grant-seekers should make *their* business, as well.

As the tidal forces that alter the nonprofit world change, funding may balloon—to match inflation or surpass it—for programs whose goals and methods have remained relatively unchanged for a relatively long period of time, which has been the recent general trend. Funding also may shrink significantly, triggering changes in basic goals and methods and inspiring a fresh "market" for nonprofit funds—which is my own reading of the current trend. Dwelling in tears-in-the-beer fashion over worst-case scenarios is a good way to get a migraine, but not a very good way to raise money. It's more helpful to gauge the strength and direction of the currents and to try to catch a helpful swell, wave or wavelet.

Generally, the big picture looked like this in 1980–81: The billions the government was spending each year on programs administered as grants or contracts certainly exceeded $100 billion, but it's hard to gauge by how much. Most of that money had specific targets before it was voted through. The grant-seekers, of course, are searching for programs where competition is at least possible, and in each such instance competition will be keen. The percentage of *discretionary* funding by corporations, private and operating foundations is proportionately higher, but their *total* spending is far less—a mere (by contrast) $4 to $6 billion. (Corporation spending now outstrips foundation spending, although only slightly, and corporations are spending roughly one-fifth to one-quarter of what the IRS is prepared to let them deduct. Obviously, this is an area that deserves the intense attention it is getting from the wisest professional fundraisers.)

A recent exchange of views in *The New York Times* detailed the way things had changed in fine arts funding, even before the federal threat. The *Times* music critic Donal Henahan bewailed the disappearance of the old-style patron, the kind who built opera houses with their names on them and covered the company's deficits forever, *à la Citizen Kane* and his opera-singer girlfriend. A keen observer of the nonprofit funding scene, Waldemar A. Nielsen *(The Big Foundations)*, replied that the money is still around, but that it's being spent in different ways by different people. Things have changed.

Nielsen noted that the old patrons, who followed European models of high culture, have been replaced by the on-staff fundraisers, creators of the "Subscribe Now!" campaigns found throughout the world of fine-arts funding. The fundraisers' new target, Nielsen said, is a consumer middle class willing to foot the same bills the millionaires once picked up. While extending consolation to potentially starving artists, Nielsen accurately described the current scene, writing: "Organized philanthropy has become Calvinist, conscience-ridden, technocratic and bureaucratized. Most of all it has become painfully infected with social scientism. It has contracted a bad case of what could be called sociologist's foot."

"Sociologist's foot" is why *parameters* and *interfaces* and *dialoguing* crop up in proposals from lyric poets who really only want a little money to wander around the Lake Country. Perhaps instead they can receive funds to interface their skills with the ghetto or the assembly line, dialoguing with those most in need of lyric poetry and turning out a sonnet or two on the side. The prevailing spirit is one of utilitarianism—the demonstrably and immediately *useful* . . . the audible, visible bang for the buck.

This same hard-nosed thinking is reflected in the recent defection of some of public television's biggest, richest friends, the corporations that once supported high-class shows with only a few words of acknowledgment in the front and end credits. Mobil, for instance, discovered that it could produce very similar, high-class materials more cheaply itself, secure an audience for them on *commercial* television and work in a couple of spot breaks that help sell its products or political ideas in a way forbidden on public television. Now, with public TV's grudging assent, legislation to allow advertising—tasteful, brief, uplifting and overseen—on public television is being considered. Things change.

As America begins its fourth Republican administration in twelve years, the Democratic opposition, as exemplified by Jerry Brown, preaches an era of lowered expectations. Few Democrats on the national scene today will stand up for federal beneficence as preached by that party's late, happy warrior, Senator Hubert H. Humphrey. Things change.

Private foundations are usually the fortunes of dead people, managed as though the founders had somehow taken it with them, which means conservative investments—the stock market. The misfortunes of a go-go market that turned going-going-gone has flattened the income of many such small foundations. But, hark! The Dow Jones industrial average nudges, then surpasses, the 1,000 mark. Will it stay there? Will foundation coffers swell once more? Things change.

But the factor-of-many-factors, the tide that the futurists at Herman Kahn's Hudson Institute once named "the long-term multifold trend" has, of late, sprung from a penny-pinching mood. Just as federal government begins to ask local governments to take over in many endeavors, the local governments have been slapped with tax revolts even in places like California and Massachusetts, hardly cockpits of conservatism. Some social scientists read these revolts not as an attack upon the programs that lose their funding, nor upon their beneficiaries, but on government mismanagement of the programs.

In some cases, the very threat of cutbacks can lead to more inventive and efficient ways of doing the same work. An urban planner of my acquaintance explained to me recently how the prospect, not the reality, of federal cutbacks had caused her organization to reconsider its whole approach. She works for an outfit funded by many regional governments and taxing authorities, each of which has its own separate needs and desires for federal money. Even her organization's role as the local "A-95 clearinghouse," an overseer function required in much federal funding and described in the Handbook section of this volume, gives it no funding veto over the authorities that collectively control it. Her organization's survival answer is several answers:

- To combine programs so that many problems and solutions are sheltered by the same technique and gain a kind of collective security from one another.

- To come up with services that will be demanded (if not paid for with cash on the barrelhead) by novel sources of funding for such a government agency, namely local corporations who stand to profit by using the agency's excellent research.

- To take the agency's findings and suggestions past the desks of the representatives within each local government who have been expected to pass them along. The agency figures it can get the word out directly, even to lower- and non-management types and thereby become indispensable. Whether the axe falls or not, there's a perception within this woman's agency that the time has come to hustle. Hustle, it appears, is what the taxpayers want to see more of.

How does it feel when the axe *really* falls?

New York City's Department of Cultural Affairs has the second-biggest arts budget in the country, after the National Endowment for the Arts. (The once-plump New York State Council on the Arts has gone on the Albany Diet.) Early in 1980, after running New York City during its harrowing brush with bankruptcy, Mayor Edward Koch pondered the bottom line, thought realistically and lowered the budgetary expectations of his Department of Cultural Affairs. The resulting program budget was to be one-*tenth* of its former self. Whether the mayor was canny enough to foresee what would happen, I cannot say. The people in the cultural affairs department were ordered not to question his wisdom in public places like, say, City Council.

In Council chambers the members' eyes bugged out as they looked, borough by borough, at lists of programs that would sink out of existence: street theater, music, galleries, classes. These were places where they had sat in free seats, attended openings, been seen . . . *campaigned.* These politicians were nervous and, according to one observer, the people who actually ran the programs were "hysterical."

Politics saved the day. With little or no protest from the mayor—it was out of *his* hands—the Council restored many of the cuts. But big cuts remained and while ordinarily you might expect a bureaucracy to react by protecting itself and letting its clients go hungry, that's not what happened here.

The mayor's philosophical approach to proposing the cuts had been a sort of local version of the New (meaning smaller) Federalism—let others step in. The men and women who ran the actual, operating programs funded by the Cultural Affairs Department feared what I just mentioned—a hungry super-agency that would let its clients go hang in order to keep its own doors open. After all, two-thirds of its payroll was gone, but this merely reflected a political decision that already had been made. In effect, the Cultural Affairs office was Sanforized, pre-shrunk, and its surviving executives assigned to the task of helping program clients stay in business. Some of the services the on-staff administrators had carried out were subcontracted, in some cases to the client field organizations that were judged to need the money more. Then they scanned existing subsidized projects along with proposals for new ones, after which they supplied funding that seemed *realistic.* They guessed, correctly, that with the city's imprimatur, many of the groups could raise more money on their own. As one of the Department's senior officials told me, "Fewer and fewer people have to be convinced that spending money on the arts is good.

"Instead of competing with them, we withdrew. We were funding 100 percent of very few things anyway. Our grants aren't matching grants, but they're like catalysts—the *Good Housekeeping* Seal of Approval for people looking for money within New York." When programs were fully supported by the Department, the goal all along had been for the city to get out, fast. Example: the New York Philharmonic's outdoor performances. Subsidized one hundred percent from city funds at first, the taxpayer share quickly plummeted to one-sixth of the total budget. (The public was paying at the ticket office.)

And even during its worst fiscal crisis, the New York City arts operation reached out to a category of support its politically-connected staff and rooters could understand and use: corporations. Through a couple of very large grants, one from a bank and one from a conglomerate, the Mayor's once-doomed Cultural Affairs unit finished out what threatened to be a bleak year in high-rise splendor, operating from its own new headquarters building on Columbus Circle, an example of corporate largesse which would have infuriated taxpayers had they been forced to pay for it. By reading the signals well in advance, by understanding how things were going to *change*, the New York City cultural effort hardly felt the axe at all. Client agencies pitched in to take over more of their own funding, not because the alternative was oblivion but because the *realistic* alternative was the strategy the administrators had been inventive enough to suggest and make work.

Of course, the real beneficiaries were projects which already had been receiving city funds—the ones considered to be "grandfathered" in, as the saying goes. Another general rule within the larger trend of fewer government dollars is that the programs already in place when the cuts come tend to fare best. In some cases, administrators adopt the old accounting rule of "last in, first out," nudging out of the picture the very projects that feel themselves to have had the hardest time getting the money they needed.

There are those who believe that the blessed rain never falls upon them, that big money—especially corporate money—plays old, safe favorites. Some of them have set out to prove it, and the figures they have compiled in scholarly fashion suggest that their argument is correct. They are minorities: blacks, Latinos, women, Asian-Americans, Native Americans, gays. The money is mostly white, mostly male, mostly apple-pie Middle-American. One out of every three *hundred* foundation trustees is a minority. More than a third of the country's foundations have no woman trustee.

These figures come from the National Committee for Responsive Philanthropy*, which, simply put, exists to spread the money around. Environmentalists, poor people, old people, the disabled—all, NCRP convincingly claims, get short-changed. The importance of this group, and others like it, is likely to increase during the present major shift in nonprofit fund-

---

*National Committee for Responsive Philanthropy, 810 18th Street, N.W., Washington, DC 20006. (202) 347-5340.

ing patterns, and for administrators intelligent enough to swallow their prejudices and analyze the Committee's figures, the way things must change should look fairly clear. And changes probably will happen, whether or not as a result of legislation.

Consider: In 1980 the Committee published a study that documents how much secrecy remains in the world of nonprofit giving. As I've already mentioned, and as you'll learn in more detail in the chapter on prospect research, the government requires foundations to reveal the financial side of their operations as part of tax exemption. But the reported figures still permit considerable secrecy about the foundation's specific goals in each grant and how the decision was made. In fact, all that the government seems interested in learning is whether a private foundation has really spent five percent of its assets (or all of its income) within a given year, as law requires. By and large, the IRS has agreed with the assertions of philanthropists like J. Howard Pew: "I'm not telling anybody anything. It's my money, isn't it?"

The National Committee for Responsive Philanthropy would like to see the government make foundations like Mr. Pew's open up their board memberships and decision-making processes before the IRS grants them new or continued tax exemption. That proposal will be fought tooth-and-nail by the families and corporations who exist alongside the dead people's money embodied in, and administered by, most of those foundations. Presently, foundations don't have to say what their purpose is (except in broad terms such as: "to promote the public good"), reveal their favored means of operation, or how and why they decide to support one project but not another—even in cases where factors like race or sex appear to be the only difference between winners and losers.

If the Committee had its way, foundations would be forced by law to reveal:

- Not just the name of a trustee, but who he or she really *is* and where they are. Implicit: the right to contact them individually.

- Whether the foundation has a paid staff to help make decisions.

- How often the board meets.

- The foundation's written policy for handling conflicts of interest.

- Whether or not the foundation has adopted an affirmative-action policy.

What the Committee is saying is: if the money is kept from the government by virtue of its alleged use for the public good, prove it.

Meanwhile, they're organizing. And, the way things change, they may have an excellent chance. I mentioned earlier the existence of an abundance of corporate money that the IRS is willing to allow as tax-deductible, but which the companies choose not to expend. Significant pressure to satisfy minority demands may result in brand-new sources of funding for groups that long have been forced to act very politically in raising their budgets. One result of that situation is the funding of projects that are perhaps more political than the people supporting them would like. The current Congressional climate may be sufficient to see the NCRP's proposals stopped short of law, but the lobbying and educational effort may result in limited early gains that prove agreeable to both sides of the fundraising equation.

Things *do* change.

Givers

Now I would like to show you some close-ups of people who give money away, intended to reveal what goes on in their heads and to give you the idea of them as *people*. As I've warned repeatedly, the administrators who read your grant proposals will be different people from these, but people, nonetheless—not computers or disembodied public laws. The truth is that the people reading your proposal are very much like yourself——men and women who share an interest in your field and who, to a greater or lesser extent than you, have made it their profession. In some cases you will find them passionately devoted to the decisions they have made on your behalf, and the example that comes to mind now is of a civil servant who, unwittingly but actually, risked his life to defend such a decision.

I had never met the man, but he had sent the organization I worked for many, many thousands of government dollars. He administered a federal program in which some of the recipients were school districts and others—like mine—were independent organizations that went to considerable pains to qualify for this kind of support. This administrator liked the breezy-but-serious approach our grants staff adopted whenever we asked for his help in threading the government maze. He liked, as well, the notion that programs could be devised that satisfied the law he administered, but managed at the same time to break new ground in public educational broadcasting, his field.

Because we scrupulously followed the law he administered, the money he gave us survived not only routine audits and a couple of surprise inspections, but it actually went to work doing what our proposals had promised. With this administrator, we managed to build up the all-important momentum I discussed earlier, in which each new project is based upon the demonstrated success of its predecessor.

Then one day, the call from Capitol Hill came. A group of Congressmen was interested in how the government was spending its money these days. It wanted to hear from our helpful administrator. On the stand. Under oath. No subpoena would be necessary, of course, and the office of the Secretary of his Cabinet Department would be happy—indeed eager—to help him prepare for his appearance. There were some books and records the Committee members would like to see. And so on.

It was literally all for the record: the *Congressional Record,* where I read the exchange, and the motive of the politicians was to reveal that government money had been expended to support a chain of public radio stations that actually provided coverage and commentary on issues like war and racism and, furthermore, gave prominent attention to left-wing views on these matters. The Congressmen felt that even if the FCC chose to license such stations, the U.S. Office of Education was not under any obligation to actually *support* them.

Did the administrator realize—asked committee counsel—that this radio station had, with government money he had sent us, broadcast the word of Godless communists? (Also the words of Republican County Central Committee members and even the Ku Klux Klan, who had a regular show, but none of *these* broadcasts was mentioned. Congressmen from the committee chairman's corner of Florida hadn't been near the Klan in *years*.)

The administrator told committee members that we met the criteria established by public law, met the standards of the FCC, which had licensed us, and to which, because its discretionary powers in such cases were greater, the complaining Congressmen might more profitably turn. He did not reveal, of course, that he had notified us once or twice at the end of a fiscal year when leftover funds were lying around in need of applications, but a call like that lay well within his discretionary powers, and the law as well.

It really didn't matter what he said, because the Congressmen were intent on the public humiliation of a public servant who had served some politicians' idea of an improper public. After allegations that the Congressmen's aides had combed from right-wing publications were placed in the *Record*, for later citation by more right-wing publications, our friend, the humane bureaucrat, was dismissed from the stand.

The politicians had wanted the man to suffer, and he suffered a heart attack. Very shortly after leaving the stand, he was in the hospital. Our organization sent flowers, and our president made a personal call, and the ending was happy. The administrator recovered and went back to work and continued to make grants just as he had done before his committee appearance. The Congressmen got their pages in the *Congressional Record*, and our friend learned that there were people who didn't like what he did out there watching him.

The point is that grant administrators in a variety of situations, not just in the government, but in corporations and foundations as well, often have many more goals and motives in common with the people asking them for money than with the people whose money they're giving away.

Sometimes grant administrators lose their jobs for doing them the way their conscience dictates. This is what happened to a foundation executive whom I met only once, but whose work was a legend within the field. His firing earned a most sympathetic story from *The New York Times*, played under a four-column headline.

This man was considered a very strong foundation director, one who quite literally directed the whole enterprise, making any required explanations afterward, if necessary, to his board of directors. The house where he presided was a few steps east of Fifth Avenue in its wealthiest latitudes, the neighborhood around the Metropolitan Museum, Jackie O's stomping grounds. In the 19th century, the foundation's headquarters had been the mansion of a noted robber baron. Now, in a satisfying twist of fate, the organization sheltered there spent its money with extraordinary boldness and social concern.

Much of that money poured into grassroots, multi-racial projects in the deep South, where the foundation director had been a veteran of the earliest and most harrowing years of the civil rights struggle. When he agreed to meet me, I was optimistic. The project I was working for was multi-racial, located in the South and was designed to touch many of the same concerns his foundation had spent money upon in the past.

As I walked into the mansion's marble foyer, I was struck immediately by the exquisite surroundings: paintings in ornate, museum-style gilt frames, rare tapestries, sculpture. It was hard to remember that money flowed from here, in trickles or torrents, to the unlikeliest places. Little black churches. Dirt-poor communities of Native Americans. Bold bands of lawyers who brought plaintiffs' cases on behalf of the poor.

The director himself, when I reached his office, turned out to be a rather plain-looking man with a kind face, and the first few minutes of our conversation were about the South in general. This led to a recitation of the things the foundation had been supporting recently, followed by an almost equally impressive list of projects he had been obliged to turn down for lack of funds to dispense. His enthusiasm for these lost causes was contagious, and he was well down the list before I realized that he was telling me, in an oblique and rather courtly fashion, that my project was among the losers.

This particular foundation director felt it necessary to tell the people he turned down exactly how the decision was reached and to demonstrate other equally worthy, or worthier, ideas that weren't funded either. And he did more. He quickly recited a list of other funding bodies to which my group could turn and agreed to supply a foot in the door with some of them. Throughout the conversation, his deep emotional commitment to winners and losers alike was plain. I walked out of the mansion with as much respect for him as I would have had if he had given me a check instead of a turn-down.

When I saw the item in the paper saying the director had resigned from the foundation after about twenty years of service, it struck me how painful the separation must have been for him. The story said he had tried to quit a couple of years earlier after disagreements with his board, but the directors had urged him to take a long sabbatical to "regain his bearings."

The disagreement was over grants he was making, the article said. He had begun to spend the Foundation's money on people who criticized America's role as arms exporter, meddler in foreign governments and supporter of dictatorial regimes. One of the groups he had helped was the Institute for Policy Studies in Washington, D.C., which lost a key staff member in a bombing conducted by the repressive and unelected government of Chile. The foundation directors were embarrassed to be connected with that Institute.

When the director returned from his sabbatical, his differences with the board remained, quickly surfaced, and his resignation was accepted. The president of the foundation's board told *The New York Times* that he, presumably unlike his departed executive director, considered the United States "one of the most moral of nation states," and a board member from the founding family assured the paper that the organization would remain liberal.

And it has. The foundation will find worthy recipients it is more comfortable with, and the projects favored by its former executive director will find their constituencies, too. His case demonstrates that not even the most secure reputation nor acclaimed record of achievement will make the directors forget whose money it is—or, at any rate, once was. Powerful though these intermediaries may sometimes be, when they overstep their role as intermediary, they risk the role itself.

Very few of the very rich choose, in the manner of Kurt Vonnegut, Jr.'s fictional Eliot Rosewater, to do the handing-out themselves. A recent collective biography of the Rockefeller family spent much of its last section detailing the story of that family's "cousins," the guilt-stricken third and fourth generations, and their efforts to reconcile their charities with their consciences. It paints them as quite the most interesting members of the wealthy clan. (One such Rockefeller cousin, Abby, devoted considerable personal struggle, as well as cash, on the Clivus Multrum, an unwieldy device for transforming human household waste into gardening mulch. It has so far failed to capture the public imagination.) Peter Collier and David Horowitz, the Rockefeller biographers, predict that in a generation or so the fortune will fan out, like a river delta, into manageable streams of money.

A friend of mine inherited a regular torrent of cash—a manufacturing company with an annual gross the size of a small country's economy. As some of the Rockefeller cousins chose to do, he adopted the strategy of living far from the family seat, working hard to achieve the anonymity made possible by his much plainer and less-famous name.

Living comfortably under what might be described as shallow but successful cover, he went to work for starvation wages with a nonprofit organization whose goals and people he came to like. He began slipping the executive director a few thousand anonymous dollars every now and then, just when it was needed most.

Staff cuts loomed, and a staff committee formed to analyze the budget and critique the management. Curious contributions were discovered in the ledgers. Somebody or some*thing* with an uncanny knowledge of the operation had been stepping in to avert crises, again and again. Who might this be? Was there some dark purpose behind the pattern—or, better yet, even more money? The staff committee demanded that the executive director forget about anonymity and name the donor.

The executive director refused. Anonymous is anonymous. But in their unhappiness over the budget cuts, the question seemed to everybody on staff to be terribly important—almost existential. Finally, so much time and energy was being expended on this minor mystery that my friend decided to step forward. At a staff meeting where demands to know the name had become intense, he raised his hand and said, "Excuse me, but I know who gave it. It was *me.*" A couple of people laughed, forcing him to explain the source of his income and, embarrassingly, his inability or unwillingness to spend even more to save those of his colleagues who were slated to lose their jobs.

Things were never again the same for him there, and in a short while he found a new and more comfortable place to work.

A few years ago in San Francisco, a group of wealthy young people like my friend banded together as the Vanguard Foundation. They had grown up in the New Left environment of the 1960s, in which the rhetoric mentioned, again and again, the "vanguard" of the revolution everybody half-hoped for. Of course, better than almost anybody, these particular kids realized there wouldn't be any revolution, but why shouldn't there be a vanguard?

This unusual group has told its own story in a book* that advises others like themselves how to use their money for good works while retaining their sanity. (Naturally, it makes interesting reading for grant writers and other fundraisers, who must account for most of its sales.) Written democratically in the second person, as though the reader were as flush as the authors, the book explains how "People will invite you to 'parties' that are really fundraisers; others will make it their business to get to know you on a friendly basis. . . . In short, you'll be asked to fill an entire spectrum of heartrending and sometimes whacky needs that have nothing to do with projects you want to fund. You may wonder, 'Am I really this popular?' The answer is no."

On his own, my friend has managed to become more comfortable with his occasional role as Lord Bountiful. For one thing, as the years go by he has started picking favorites and sticking with them. "I don't feel guilty about saying no now." And what about the occasional project that fails? "If you're giving to the right things, you should expect failure now and then."

Sitting alone in his office, going over the requests, and sitting on the boards of foundations, what kind of proposals does he see? "Band-Aids, things that are service-oriented, that stop the problem from hurting, not things that will really change the situation." The older foundations, he believes, love Band-Aids—and the bigger the better. "Their role, in some re-

---

Robin Hood Was Right. $5 from Vanguard Public Foundation, 4112 24th Street, San Francisco CA 94114.

spects, is to keep the lid on some of the pressures, not to direct those pressures."

Because he volunteers his own fund-raising clout and skills to some of the groups he chooses to help, he has an interesting view of both teams playing the grants game—the givers and the takers. He recalled to me recently how a foundation with a very liberal reputation turned down a proposal he had worked hard to match with the foundations's goals and funding pattern: "They just took the letter we sent them and scribbled on the bottom, 'Sorry—this doesn't meet our needs at this time.' Some of the most liberal ones give you the biggest runaround."

And his vantage point gives special weight to his answer to the eternal fundraising question: Is it what you've got or who you know?

"Who you know."

"By what percentage?"

"Seventy-five to twenty-five."

●

A bureaucrat, a foundation director, a millionaire who gives it away personally. Nothing that happened in my first brushes with these three men prepared me for the people they actually turned out to be—not simply individuals who had the power to say yea or nay to a project I sought funds for, but human beings with human needs and concerns.

To win the grants game, you must meet and truly come to know many scores, even hundreds, of men and women like these. At the point in your relationship when these individuals come to be more important than the money they represent, the converse will probably be true for them: you'll be more important than the project in your proposal.

Then both sides of the game are in the magical arena where conversation and compromise match or outweigh the importance of a tight budget or a stunningly written project summary. Because people give money to people, winning the grant from people you know will be especially sweet. And in those cases when you lose, the bitterness of defeat may be tempered a little and your chances may be greater for funding the next time around.

Takers

I almost hesitate to introduce you to these final two characters, a couple of takers you could categorize as sharpies. But I want to wrap up the "human" half of this book by celebrating the combination of energy and imagination they represent—that joyful spirit I mentioned as helpful to anyone playing any game at all.

The first was an assistant professor of English at a time like now, when there were too many assistant professors of English. He wanted research grants at a time when research grants were going to minority applicants and impacted areas and there he was: white, male, and with one of the most white, male subjects imaginable. I'll say for purposes of this tale that his subject was the 19th century Scottish writer Thomas Carlyle.

Conducting prospect research, the young assistant professor saw how few grants went to individuals, how many were sent to institutions and organizations. He wasn't far enough up in the English Department pecking order to get the chairman's signature on his proposals because if any grants were to be written around this particular English Department, they were going to full professors, the way God intended.

Then, looking at lists of grants made, our hero noticed that many prominent, dead literary figures had Societies—or as a tax accountant might put it: fully tax-deductible nonprofit associations—dedicated to their memories. So the young assistant professor became the founder of the Thomas Carlyle Society. Other Carlyle scholars were anxious to join, once the flow of grants had begun. In a field where publication (which means tenure, which means happiness) appeared throttled because the tides were running the other way, coffers opened. If they haven't started such a scholarly society in your field of endeavor, you'll be happy to know the Handbook that follows this section includes complete details on how to proceed.

I'll call the subject of my final close-up Mark. He and a handful of friends were finishing a very late dinner one night a couple of years ago when he glanced at his watch: 10:30 PM.

"What day is this?" he cried.

"The thirtieth," replied a well-informed dinner guest.

In a moment of horrific illumination, Mark realized that the postmark deadline for applications to the National Endowment for the Arts was less than two hours away.

Was it possible?

Why not try?

Mark is a lawyer involved in the fine and public arts: art in the streets, street life in the gallery, that sort of thing. The project at hand was a scheme to convert an attractively empty warehouse into a large gallery and performance space before it drifted back to being just a warehouse again.

"You have to have a gimmick," Mark explains, and in this case the gimmick was almost Buddhistic in its simplicity: emptiness, the notion of a vast sheltering space for any number of arts organizations. No costly and troublesome stages or walls or offices to make it look like a theater or gallery or concert hall or classroom. Simply *emptiness*—all things to all people.

Personally, I disagree that a gimmick is necessary to get the grant, but sometimes it helps, and in this case it provided the lead element for the project narrative, which Mark set to work writing. A dinner guest was given a stack of budgets from previous years and told to be rather conservative with the new one. Could he have it finished in, say, half an hour? Yet another guest was dispatched to cull boxes of old slides for examples of the kinds of big art and performance the warehouse might feature.

The minutes raced by, but the dinner wine had been kind, and Mark's prose was a rhapsody, singing of the small arts operations that would find succor and shelter beneath the warehouse roof, describing the long-term support of his organization by the California Arts Council, painting a vivid picture (and enclosing proof through newspaper clippings and letters of commendation already on file) of an art project so plugged into its total community that it fairly crackled and hummed in anticipation of the federal money to come.

Fortunately, the Post Office was only twelve blocks from Mark's loft, and even more fortunately, because he works where he lives he had a photocopy machine right in the kitchen. By 11:45 PM everyone had completed their part of the grant proposal. Mark swiftly keyed their pages and exhibits to the appropriate blanks in the application form, Xeroxed everything, slapped what struck him as too much postage on the envelope and raced (or *was* raced; by then he was too strung-out to drive himself) to the night window at the Post Office.

Evidently it was coffee-break time. Nobody responded to the night-bell, to his pounding on the window.

It was 11:58, then midnight.

Finally the window creaked open and a slightly surly postal worker asked what all the fuss was about.

"This application! It has to be postmarked by midnight, or we go out of business!"

"Well, you're out of luck, son," the postal worker explained, going on to reveal that except for once a year—April 15th—the cancellation machines were set ahead to the next day's date well before the midnight coffee break.

"Oh, God—*please,*" Mark implored, and the worker, caught up in the infectious, get-the-government aspect of it all, went on a reconnaissance of the parcel post windows and returned with a battered old handstamp that still carried yesterday's date. With a big grin, he stamped cancellations all over Mark's fat envelope, and, a couple of months later, the check for $5,000 arrived, one of the speckled blue kind I mentioned on the first page of this book.

Is this any way to get a grant?

Yes and no. No, of course, because it would have been more sensible to get to work a little earlier—say, three in the afternoon. But yes, because he got the money. (Not through dumb luck or even through personal connections with the National Endowment for the Arts; he'd never met the people, not even their local scout, although as a recipient he got to know them better in succeeding years, and as they grew to believe more and more in the idea he had described in his proposal and executed with finesse, he got more and more of their money.)

Mark won the grants game because he had spent a long time getting ready to write the successful application. He had lobbied the embryo California Arts Council as it came into being, before it even had staff members.

When staff members finally came aboard, he and his colleagues at the gallery were veritable Methuselahs to them, the most grandfatherly of grandfathered projects. Many bodies, NEA and the California Arts Council included, adopt an informal rule of not helping a project until it has achieved three full years of operations on its own. By pluck and luck, Mark had done so.

His grant proposal was reassuring. The letters of support it contained were real, the product of genuine community connections Mark had developed during the struggling early years of the project. The clippings and reviews were real, serious attention from arts journalists and reviewers describing exhibits the gallery already had sheltered.

Through years of effort and careful record-keeping and documentation salted away for just such a minor crisis as the forgotten deadline, Mark had come to know—and to be able to prove—why they were going to give him the money. His proposal indeed did, as recommended, read as though the folks at the National Endowment for the Arts had written it themselves, and they read its successors with equal eagerness.

"The secret was in the files," Mark explains. "It all gets down to how good the files are. You pull out your files and plug in what you need.

"The first time you look at it, it's overwhelming. You just look at it and look at it and turn away from it. It's easy to make excuses not to get into it."

And so Mark had made excuses that lasted until ninety minutes before deadline, and his first draft of the grant proposal was the only draft.

Only a fool—or, as in this case, a genius—would become procrastination's toy to this extent. But Mark was right. The secret *is* the files, and the rest of this book is about how to fill them up.

Shall we play?

Part Two:

THE GRANTS HANDBOOK

First of All:
Can this Project be Funded?

The grants game is a big, complicated process you can simplify with effective planning, and this handbook will show you how. But before you even scan the chapters ahead on creating your own grant system, you should ask yourself some hard questions about your project.

As you do so, keep in mind that well over 90 percent of all grant proposals fail. Is the gap between need and funding really that great?

No. The truth is, most proposals are shots in the dark, letters to Santa; requests that the money managers spot right away as less-than-serious, less than well-planned. In the blunt word these money managers often employ, most of the ideas are "ratholes."

Before you waste their time (and much more of your own), ask yourself the four questions below. It may be painful to answer any of them "no," but in the super-competitive world of the grants game, even a *qualified* "yes" may not be good enough. The answer to each of these questions needs to be a resounding "yes" that jumps right off the pages of your proposal.

Is your project real?

Some applicants say, "Yes, if we get the money." But what if you don't? Would you look for other sources of cash, throw bake sales, make a personal sacrifice like selling your car?

It may sound paradoxical, but the project likeliest to get the money is the one likeliest to succeed *without* the money. The proposal reader is looking for applicants who know that most nonprofit undertakings are funded by a broad variety of sources and are propelled by ongoing work that demands continued support on the basis of earlier successes.

The proposal you write must:

- Describe the project.

- Set forth the work and life experiences of the people involved.

- Reveal its budget and funding.

- Satisfy legal requirements.

- Name reassuring names as mentors and sponsors.

It has to do that job in a just-the-facts, plain-vanilla way in which the solidity of your planning, not the shape of your prose style, ranks first. One or two of these key elements may be stronger than others, but none can be missing if you really expect the money.

Do you have the cold, hard facts that will make your proposal look real on paper? *Is* your project real?

Is your project reasonable?

A subtler question, but equally important. It's a question you hear sometimes in courts of law: "What would the *reasonable* person have done?" The money managers who read your proposal are looking for a *reasonable* balance between problem (or goal) and solution.

For example, suppose that the problem is rampant bankruptcy among lower-income families in your city. If you propose a debt clinic that will eliminate the problem, you're promising too much. If you set out a reasonable goal for *reducing* bankruptcies—perhaps based on statistics from a program somewhere else—a local corporate foundation might accept the reasonableness of the idea and fund it.

Good managers sometimes say their goal is the total elimination of surprise from their operation. Grant readers want management like that for the money they give away—people who won't surprise them with follow-up reports that document failure because they promised too much in the first place. (Even worse, naive recipients who are *themselves* surprised by the gap between promise and performance.)

Grants game newcomers sometimes bite off more than they can chew in their attempt to deliver the biggest bang for the buck. Whether you're an individual recipient or guiding a team effort, the money you're seeking will not result in a quantum leap in your effort. Life will be very much the same on either side of the check. Plan accordingly—*reasonably.*

Is your project well-planned?

The essential grants-game equation says problem + solution = money. But seeing the problem and proposing the solution aren't enough. The detailed *planning* of the solution is often the deciding factor, especially in cases when givers have called for proposals and the competing applicants know they're in effect bidding on performing a job to specifications.

Is your work plan *the* way to get the job done? Are you and your colleagues, if any, exactly the right people to do that job? Does your budget show extraordinary good sense about managing other people's money?

If your project is brand-new to you and you can't plan on the basis of your own experience, prove to the proposal reader that you've investigated other very similar projects and have taken their success (or failure) into account in your own plans. Ask prospective donors for their ideas on planning, and list mentors and sponsors whose own rich experience in your field validates your planning.

Thinking competitively may mean a proposal that is more efficient, costs less to fund or is better-staffed than the next applicant's. That can be the difference between winning and losing. Advantages in all three categories could guarantee success. *Is* your project well-planned?

Is your project sheltered?

Money loves company, not only the company of other sources of money but of institutions and organizations which shelter and oversee grant recipients. The smaller you are, the more you need shelter: the informal shelter of institutional or personal association, the formal shelter of nonprofit associative or corporate identity, or a program to be administered directly by an organization with a track record.

Corporate and small foundations, which represent the likeliest funding targets for individuals and small organizations, usually operate with small or part-time staffs, and they are most comfortable when their money is being spent by organizations that are large and familiar to them. Such recipients offer a quality of management the small foundation desires but can't handle alone. Except for a handful of research and arts grants, government money goes almost exclusively to such shelters.

If your project seems to be standing alone, disconnected from others whose history or resources would suggest collaboration or guidance, the decision-makers may ask you very directly why you've chosen to go it alone. Can you convince them it's necessary?

In some cases, laws or internal rules may absolutely restrict a donor's gifts to government bodies, to institutions of a certain size, to organizations that have been in existence for a certain number of years before applying. Some tax-deductible organizations are more tax-deductible than others (20 percent more, to be precise), and some donors give only to the so-called "public" charities, those supported by a relatively large number of relatively small contributions.

Finding out about these restrictions and preferences is a key part of prospect research. Satisfying them may require a major change in the way you think about your project. You may have to get in the shade of a larger organization, or through fairly simple legal paperwork actually become a tax-deductible nonprofit association or corporation. If you're already tax-exempt, you may want to increase your public fund-raising in order to qualify for more money by becoming more attractively deductible.

This handbook describes the full range of shelter available to you, and how to seek it. But right now, before you start, *is* your project sheltered?

If you said *yes* to all four of these questions, you look like a winner right out of the gate.

If you had to qualify your answer, or answer *no* to any of them, use the chapters ahead to strengthen your position.

Now it's time to build your own grant system.

Organizing Your Grant System

This handbook breaks down the big job of writing a grant proposal into smaller jobs you can handle one at a time. It also shows you how to set up and maintain a system of continuous prospect research and how to organize the equally essential person-to-person aspects of successful nonprofit fund-raising.

There is no such thing as an ideal form of grant proposal. Some givers, especially the government, require you to follow intricate forms of their own. Others leave it up to you, and what you know of their program and motives will guide the final form and style you use with them.

But all proposals have several broad elements in common. This handbook identifies them, breaks them down into sub-tasks, and allows you to go to work right now. This system will allow you to identify urgent tasks that can block submission if they don't get done on time, and it will give you quick access to small bits of work you can handle in a spare moment.

The resulting set of files will help you create fresh, tailor-made proposals as your prospect research reveals new sources of money. And because all proposals are collaborative to some extent, the guidelines will show you how to direct the work of contributing associates and to secure the help you may need from outside sources, such as sponsors or official agencies.

From start to finish, keep in mind that . . .

A GRANT PROPOSAL IS SIMPLY A PAPERWORK SYSTEM FOR SETTING FORTH THE MERITS OF YOUR PROJECT IN THE CLEAREST, MOST CONCISE AND MOST PERSUASIVE FORM POSSIBLE.

How to use this handbook

The chapters that follow are arranged along the lines of the four major elements of successful, ongoing nonprofit fundraising:

1. *Prospect research.* How to find prospects for your grant proposal, analyze their value to you and choose the ones worth pursuing.

2. *The case statement and its supplements.* How to complete the pages of the proposal describing the project, its setting and the qualifications of those involved.

3. *The reassurance pages.* How to show institutional and/or governmental approvals and associations, satisfaction of corporate and tax requirements, financial statements and the endorsements of official or unofficial sponsors of the specific project for which funds are sought.

4. *Compilation, submission and follow-through.* How to tag and meet deadlines for completing a proposal from materials in your files. How to transform official applications into indexes for your own. How to submit the proposal and follow its progress through the granting organization. How to negotiate out of a threatened turn-down and how to follow-up success or failure.

You will need a set of file folders to match these four main categories, and later you may need more to match the sub-tasks. If you don't have a filing cabinet, get an empty box from the grocery or buy a cardboard file box from a stationer. (The plastic bus-boxes restaurants use for dirty dishes are excellent, stackable organizers and cost only two or three dollars each at restaurant supply houses.)

Start your files immediately, even though you have nothing to put in them yet. (Later, an empty file will be a danger signal.)

The working chapters of the handbook are organized so you can scan the section headings and decide whether a particular set of tasks is necessary for the proposal or proposal-writing campaign you're undertaking. If a task is unnecessary or completed, scan ahead, stopping to follow the checklists in the text whenever necessary.

Prospect Research

The general idea

To get grants you need not only a project whose value you can demonstrate, but a good match between that project and the funding sources you're trying to convince. The link is prospect research, the job of locating the widest possible range of reasonable funding targets and analyzing them in order to focus your efforts on the most promising few.

Professional grant writers know that prospect research is as important as preparation and submission of the written proposal. Not only is writing a well-targeted and effective proposal impossible without it, prospect research provides your first direct contacts with the individuals who will later decide whether you get the money, and it helps you to make anyone assisting your effort (sponsors, advocates, board members, and so on) more deeply engaged and effective.

Prospect research isn't a one-time-only affair. It's a continuous process that should happen alongside the other tasks involved in grant writing. The groundwork stages of prospect research allow you to rehearse your proposal and the supporting materials, to change them and—ideally—to involve the decision-makers as directly as proper and possible in putting together a proposal they will say yes to.

The system in this chapter is a simplified version of the techniques most often used and taught by professional fundraisers and grant counselors.

It begins with a basic list of funding sources drawn from standard reference works, libraries, fundraising resource centers, government agencies, personal interviews and a handful of less likely, but useful, places. Then, with a one-page form, you can identify the funding targets really worth concentrating on and, in the final step, assign each a dollar goal—the amount you expect them to contribute to your project.

Throughout this process people are more important than paperwork, but you should do the paperwork even if you're using this handbook to write a proposal to a program you already know about. Grant writing is a more or less seamless continuum of tasks, and eliminating prospect analysis to get on with writing the proposal is a false economy of time. Prospect analysis is the basis for all that happens later.

The prospect analysis form

Grant writers are saddled with so much paperwork that you may question the wisdom of making a blank form of your own, but this simple sheet will give you, at a glance, a rundown on each funding prospect and, in cases where the job of grant writing is shared among several persons, make meetings and conferences on the subject flow smoothly.

Glance now at the form (Figure 1, Appendix Three) and refer to it as you read the section below on prospect analysis. After you've finished the chapter, use a typewriter and a straight-edge to make a form of your own. You may want to tailor the "grant analysis" section of the sheet to match your own project more closely. That's okay. The form is a tool, not a magic formula. Then have your version of the form duplicated. You can get a hundred copies for less than five dollars at an instant-print shop.

The form will be essential for the library work, but you also should carry blanks with you whenever possible. Meetings, conferences and chance conversations will provide clues to new sources, and a prospect sheet that's *begun* with names already written on the lines listing contacts and connections is the most valuable tool of all.

Who should conduct the prospect analysis?

The people most directly involved in the project itself. You can delegate away, or even hire out, the initial library searching that provides the basic prospect list, but the conversations and interviews that follow are too intimately connected with your prospects of success for someone else to do them.

If you have a formal board of directors or development (meaning fundraising) committee connected with your project or institution, get them involved in analyzing the grant programs for which you've compiled the basic information at the top of the sheets. And if you're working alone, go ahead and create your own informal "board of directors"—not a real committee, but the group of colleagues and supporters who stand by your project. Just as with the larger, more formal organizations, their role in prospect research translates into direct action in later stages of getting the grant, such as possible negotiations.

Developing your prospect list

The prospect list is like a shopping list. It's the biggest set of *possible* funding sources that you can put together quickly.

The tools for your search are as close as your library, and the basic references you'll find there are surprisingly complete—as far as they go. And actually, with the exception of some special collections and resource centers I'll explain shortly, that's going about as far as the listings in any other directory or catalog. You'll be able to find out about the *existence* of giving programs, but not all you need to know about their people, their private goals, their likes and dislikes.

Your own legwork will help fill in the blanks, but at the earliest stage of research the basic sources will help you find donors who:

- Give to projects with goals like yours or—better yet—*favor* ideas like yours.

- Give to projects in your geographic area. (And local sources are best, because they lie within reach of a network of influence you can construct.)

- Give on a scale that matches the scale of your project.

Checklist: prospect resources

☐ *Basic resources in libraries and special research centers.* The world of grants changes quickly, and many of the basic research materials are out of date almost as soon as they're published. Since you're always looking at information about the recent past, it's up to you to verify and update what you know about your prospects through direct contact with them. Because many of the basic references and services are expensive, individual grant applicants and small organizations usually perform their basic prospect research in libraries and special grant information centers. Appendix One to this book, Prospect Research Resources, gives a state-by-state listing of such resource collections and information on state and regional foundation directories currently in print.

   ☐ *Local public and institutional libraries.* Your local public, college or institutional library should have some of the basic resources listed just below, such as *The Foundation Directory*, together with a selection of more general books, such as this one, on the subject of grants. These guides and books may be available in general stacks as well as reference rooms, and are shelved under the Dewey Decimal System classification *Philanthropy*, 361.7 Sometimes college, university and institutional libraries (such as those at research hospitals) are open to members of the public by special arrangement or, in the case of certain state-supported institutions, by law. The more specialized resources listed ahead—the newsletters and binder services that scan the world of government grants, for example—may be available to you through the development (money-raising) or chief financial officer's office of an institution with which you're affiliated or friendly, such as a museum, school system, regional church office, or the headquarters or regional office of your union or professional association.

☐ *Foundation Center offices and cooperating collections.* Since the early 1970s The Foundation Center, supported by other foundations, has done a superb job of making sense out of the world of grants from America's 22,000-plus private foundations. Their system currently is being expanded to gather more data about the corporations and corporate foundations whose nonprofit funding surpassed that from private foundations in 1979. The Foundation Center offices in New York, Washington, D.C., Cleveland and San Francisco and 90-odd cooperating libraries and organizations, all of which are listed by state in Appendix One to this book, offer a national overview of the world of grants through the Foundation Center services and publications listed immediately ahead. In addition, even more detailed data on all 22,000 American foundations are available in the Center's Washington, D.C., and New York collections; the Center's Cleveland office shelters its raw materials on midwestern givers, and complete records on West Coast foundations are in the Center's San Francisco facility. The four Foundation Center offices and eleven other "foundation foundation" groups around the country offer special seminars on prospect research and grant-writing. To provide you with updated information about the Center and the 90 cooperating collections, the Center operates a toll-free line, (800) 424-9836, that is staffed during business hours, Eastern time. The Center also publishes a $4.95 guide, *Foundation Fundamentals*, that instructs newcomers in details of the research system.

☐ *The Foundation Directory.* Names, addresses, donors, purpose, assets, expenditures, high/low figures, officers and trustees, correspondence contact, application procedures and federal employer identification number (useful in acquiring IRS reports) for 3,138 American foundations, the largest of more than 22,000 recognized by the IRS. The eighth edition costs $45 from The Foundation Center, 888 Seventh Avenue, New York, NY 10016. The directory includes foundations that have $1 million or more in assets, or that give away $100,000 or more a year. The foundations in this book account for nine out of ten grant dollars, and the *crème de la crème,* the thousand biggest, are profiled exhaustively in a loose-leaf service called *Source Book Profiles,* which costs $200 a year from The Foundation Center. The Center updates these in-depth listings at a rate of 500 per year, 85 or so profiles every other month. Therefore, you must spend another $200 to secure the previous year's analyses and have a complete set.

Virtually all of the resource collections listed in the Appendix will have the *Profiles.* It's an especially valuable tool, because its bimonthly *Foundation Profiles Update* lists recent changes in basic information about the givers, including new trends in grant-giving patterns. The information in the *Directory,* the *Profiles* and the *Updates* will allow you to fill out most of a prospect analysis sheet on a particular source at a single sitting.

Because of the convenience of this system, many new researchers stop here. This is a big mistake. Another 18,000 foundations exist, and their mostly-local scope makes them ripe targets for the system you're building. Fortunately, a third Foundation Center publication offers you basic clues about them:

☐ *The National Data Book.* This two-volume paperback issued each November by The Foundation Center (cost: $45), lists more than 22,000 foundations alphabetically, by state and in descending order of total grants made. It *doesn't* list all officers, name contacts, reveal application procedures or analyze grants in depth, although its charts and tables do provide a remarkable overall picture of giving patterns in any particular region. But it *does* say whether a foundation issues an annual report, and the information given is enough to help you conduct a complete analysis using the methods described ahead.

☐ *Special matchmaking services.* The Foundation Center and certain of its cooperating collections offer print-outs from a computer program called COMSEARCH, that categorizes recent grants by large foundations according to more than a hundred subject categories. And the Center's *Foundation Grants Index Annual* analyzes around 20,000 grants a year by even narrower categories: recipient state, subject and "keywords."

☐ *Government grants: starting points.* Unfortunately, and perhaps because it's impossible, nothing like The Foundation Center exists to make sense out of the much bigger field of government grants. In looking for sources of government money, you must rely upon two principal categories of data:

- Special information systems, such as newsletters and networks, developed to serve your field.

- The direct advice of mentors in your field, whom you seek out.

The goal of prospect research into government grants is simple: *Find the name, address and telephone number of the person in the government who will read your proposal and have the most to say about whether you get the money.* For a first, broad overview, the government itself offers three services. Checklist items ahead tell you how to use their clues in narrowing the search.

☐ *Catalog of Domestic Federal Assistance.* This loose-leaf service costs $20 a year from the Superintendent of Documents, U.S.

Government Printing Office, Washington, DC 20402. Some agencies report what they're up to more clearly than others, but the service's Applicant Eligibility Index shows at a glance who's eligible for programs directly administered by federal agencies. Also hidden within this book are the amounts of federal funds sent to states, counties and cities for local administration—some in the form of grants—and since no similar guide to state and local giving yet exists, the catalog gives you something to wave at local officials during your search for the money's final outlet.

☐ *FAPRS: The Federal Assistance Programs Retrieval System.* Begun by the Department of Agriculture, this computerized system covers that agency's programs in detail and, because the need is there, is attempting to become an electronic (and more thorough) version of the catalog listed immediately above. Government agencies and other institutions that rely upon federal funds have terminals, and so do a growing number of libraries and resource centers, although these can be difficult to find or restricted from your use once you do. A letter to your Congressman requesting access to the nearest terminal might help, although most of the data listed (like the catalog's) is presented in baffling bureaucratese, and you may find that the trip wasn't worthwhile. (FAPRS Administrator, U.S. Department of Agriculture, Washington, DC 20250.)

☐ *Federal Information Centers and telephone tie-lines.* The government has created these centers in more than 85 American cities so far (although Alaska, North and South Dakota, Wyoming and West Virginia have none). Run by the General Services Administration, they should, in theory, help you find regional offices for programs listed in the catalog above, a contact for FAPRS access, and so on. Some provide toll-free tie-lines to regional centers with more information. To find one in your city, turn to "U.S. Government" in the white pages of your telephone book. The Federal Information Center will be listed in the box of "frequently called numbers" above the listings and in the alphabetical listings under "F," (*not* "G" for General Services Administration).

☐ *Government grants: some of the biggies.* Nobody really knows how much the government gives away each year. Estimates range upward of $100 billion for grants and contract programs, but the grants available to individuals and nonprofit organizations are far narrower, although still in the $10–30-billion range. Here is an agency-by-agency listing of the major government departments, giving you the address and phone number of the "head office," a flash-listing of those programs reported by the agencies themselves as open to individual grant applicants, nonprofit organizations, or both.

☐ *Department of Agriculture*

Headquarters: 14th Street and Independence Avenue, S.W. Washington, DC 20250, (202) 655-4000

Northeast Region: Room 333, Administration Building 003, Agricultural Research Center, Beltsville, MD 20705, (301) 344-3418

North Central Region: 2000 West Pioneer Parkway, Peoria, IL 61614, (309) 360-7176

Southern Region: 701 Loyola Avenue, P.O. Box 53326, New Orleans, LA 70153, (504) 682-6753

Western Region: 2850 Telegraph Avenue, Berkeley, CA 94705, (415) 449-3565

USDA programs open to individuals and nonprofit groups:

- Emergency Conservation Program
  - Water Bank Program
  - Agricultural Conservation Program
  - Farm Labor Housing Grants
  - Very-Low-Income Housing Repair Grants
  - Technical and Supervisory Assistance Grants

- Basic and Applied Agricultural Research
- Competitive Agricultural Research Grants

□ *Department of Commerce*

Headquarters: 14th Street and Constitution Avenue, N.W., Washington, DC 20230, (202) 783-9200

Regional offices of Economic Development Administration, the Department's principal grant-making body:

Rocky Mountain: Suite 505, Title Building, 907 17th Street, Denver, CO 80202, (303) 837-4717

Southeastern: Suite 700, 1365 Peachtree Street, N.E., Atlanta, GA 30309, (404) 881-7401

Midwestern: 175 W. Jackson Boulevard, Suite A-1630, Chicago IL 60604, (312) 353-7706

Atlantic: 10424 Federal Building, 600 Arch Street, Philadelphia, PA 19106

Southwestern: Suite 600, American Bank Tower, 221 West 6th Street, Austin TX 78701, (512) 397-5461

Western: 1700 Westlake Avenue North, Suite 500, Seattle WA 98109, (206) 442-0596

Commerce programs open to individuals and nonprofit groups include:

- Anadromous and Great Lakes Fisheries Conservation
- Sea Grant Support (NOAA)
- Minority Business Development (EDA and Regional Action Planning Commissions)

□ *Department of Education*

Headquarters: 400 Maryland Avenue, S.W., Washington, DC 20202

National Institute of Education: 1200 19th Street, Washington, DC 20208

This is one of the giants, even after its separation from the rest of the former Department of Health, Education and Welfare.

It's also one of the agencies that makes most sense when explaining itself. A mere sampling of programs open to individual and small nonprofit grant applicants includes:
- Foreign Language and Area Studies Research
- Teacher Exchange
- Fulbright-Hays Training Grants (faculty abroad)
- Fulbright-Hays Training Grants (dissertations abroad)
- Basic Educational Opportunity Grant Program
- Public Service Education Institutional Grants
- Strengthening Research Library Resources
- Graduate and Professional Opportunities
- Minority Access to Research Careers

☐ *General Services Administration*

The federal government's purchasing agent and housekeeper. It's also the records-keeper, and makes grants through its National Archives and Records Service, principally in the fields of librarianship and document research. National Historical and Records Commission, National Archives Building, Washington, DC 20408.

☐ *Department of Health and Human Services*

The rest of the old HEW. Its subsidiaries, such as the National Institutes of Health, are among the grant-making giants of the federal government.

- National Institutes of Health, Bethesda MD 20205
- Health Services Administration
- Health Resources Administration
- Ten regional offices of HHS:

John F. Kennedy Federal Building, Government Center, Boston, MA 02203, (617) 223-6830

26 Federal Plaza, Room 3835, New York, NY 10007, (212) 264-4483

3535 Market Street, Philadelphia, PA 19101, (215) 596-6421

101 Marietta Tower Building, Atlanta, GA 30323, (404) 221-2261

300 South Wacker Drive, Chicago, IL 60606, (312) 353-7800

1200 Main Tower Building, Dallas, TX 75202, (214) 767-3311

601 East 12th Street, Kansas City, MO 64106, (816) 374-2821

Federal Office Building, 1961 Stout Street, Denver, CO 80294, (303) 837-2831

Federal Office Building, United Nations Plaza, San Francisco, CA 94102, (415) 556-2246

Arcade Plaza Building, MS-803, 1321 Second Avenue, Seattle, WA 98101, (206) 442-1290

The department has operating subdivisions that conduct grant-making programs of research into eye, heart, lung, cancer, allergy, arthritis and metabolic disturbances, and so on. The *NIH Guide for Grants and Contracts*, available from NIH, Bethesda MD 20014, is free, and explains application policies for the many subdivisions administered by the Institutes.

Health and Human Services publishes a comprehensive loose-leaf service, updated regularly, that offers guidelines on the full range of its grant-making programs: *Grants Administration Manual*, $29 from Superintendent of Documents, Washington, DC 20402. Specify GPO Catalog No. HE1. 6/7

□ *Department of the Interior*

Water, wildlife and, through its Bureau of Indian Affairs, a broad-ranging grant program restricted to (and on behalf of) Native Americans; some grants administered cooperatively with tribal governments.

Headquarters: 18th and C, N.W., Washington, DC 20202, (202) 343-1100

Office of Water Research and Technology: address same as above, (202) 343-4561

Commissioner of Indian Affairs: 1951 Constitution Avenue, N.W., Room 4618, Washington, DC 20245, (202) 343-5582

☐ *Department of Justice*

Its massive Law Enforcement Assistance Administration gives its money away through and to local governments. But sub-agencies such as the National Institute for Justice and National Institute of Corrections offer grants to individuals and small nonprofit groups in their fields.

National Institute of Corrections: 320 First Street, N.W., Washington, DC 20534, (202) 724-3106

National Institute of Justice: Rockville, MD 20850

☐ *Department of Labor*

Individuals and small nonprofits qualify for its grants in employment and training and in occupational safety and health (OSHA). But its subsidiary, the Employment and Training Administration, administers the localized network of CETA grants that, evident early victims of the new government fiscal prudence, still created a remarkable network of support for small community-based organizations (or CBOs.) Pursue that network through these ETA regional offices:

Room 1707 John F. Kennedy Building, Government Center, Boston, MA 02203, (617) 223-6440

1515 Broadway, Room 3730, New York, NY 10036, (212) 399-5703

P.O. Box 8796, Philadelphia, PA 19101, (215) 596-6346

1371 Peachtree Street, N.E., Room 405, Atlanta, GA 30309, (404) 881-3691

230 South Dearborn Street, 6th Floor, Chicago, IL 60604, (312) 353-0313

555 Griffin Square Building, Room 317, Griffin and Young Streets, Dallas, TX 75202, (214) 729-6877

Federal Building, Room 1000, 911 Walnut Street, Kansas City, MO 64106, (816) 374-3796

1961 Stout Street, Denver, CO 80294, (303) 837-3031

Federal Building, 450 Golden Gate Avenue, San Francisco, CA 94102, (415) 556-7020

Room 1114, Federal Office Building, 909 First Avenue, Seattle, WA 98174, (206) 442-4695

□ *National Endowment for the Arts*

A treasure-trove of individual and small-institution fellowships in design, dance, artists-in-schools, literature, music, radio-television-film, theater, visual arts, expansion arts, folk arts, opera and musical theater, challenge grants to help museums, theaters and so on raise more local funds. These are the people to turn to after you've established a reputation for yourself. With the twin National Endowment for the Humanities, it's the most susceptible of government agencies to networks of personal influence. It uses regional talent-spotters and coordinators. Its programs are summarized and its successes celebrated in the pages of a bimonthly journal: *The Cultural Post*, $10 a year from Superintendent of Documents, Washington, DC 20402.

The Endowment publishes a *Guide to Programs*, that clarifies its stepping-stone approach to grants and the involvement of the National Council on the Arts. It's available from The National Endowment for the Arts, 2401 E Street, N.W., Washington, DC 20506, (202) 634-6369.

□ *National Endowment for the Humanities*

Scholarship, higher education, mid-career programs and research into experimental education and the promotion of the humanities are among its programs. These are open to individual applicants and small nonprofit organizations. Like its twin Arts Endowment, it publishes word of old and new programs in its bimonthly journal: *Humanities*, $7 a year from Superintendent of Documents, Washington, DC 20402.

To communicate with the Endowment itself: National Endowment for the Humanities, 806 15th Street, N.W., Washington, DC 20506, (202) 382-7465.

☐ *National Science Foundation*

Around a billion dollars a year, dispensed to every corner of science, and a rich field for individual and small nonprofit applicants in all of its areas of concern. Six subdivisions administer the grants, but an overview is available in a catalog-plus-update service that includes basic policies and procedures and regular additions as new grants are made available: NSF Grant Policy Manual, $9 a year from Superintendent of Documents, Washington, DC 20402.

The Foundation's bimonthly magazine about itself is: *Mosaic*, $10 a year from Superintendent of Documents, Washington, DC 20402.

Reach the Foundation itself at: National Science Foundation, 1800 G Street, N.W., Washington, DC 20550, (202) 655-4000.

☐ *Government and foundation grants: specialized resources.* A light industry has sprung up to cull and decipher the RFPs (requests for proposals), promulgations and statutes that guide and reveal the government's giving. (The *Commerce Business Daily* and *Federal Register* contain much of the information, but their use generally is beyond the comfortable capabilities of individual applicants and small organizations.) Some of these services cover foundation and corporate grant programs, too. The binder and newsletter services listed below are relatively costly, but tremendously thorough and useful. You should search them out in institutional libraries and development offices. Some nonprofit groups chip in to share them. If your organization can afford them, remember that subscription prices may have escalated since this book went to press. The publishers' phone numbers are included so you can check before ordering.

☐ *The Aris Funding Messenger.* The staff of the Academic Research Information System scans the whole world of government, foundation and corporate funding and makes reports in three areas of specialization: the *Medical Sciences Report* ($105 a year for eight reports, plus supplements), the *Social and Natural Sciences Report* ($105 a year for eight reports, plus supplements) and the *Creative Arts and Humanities Report* ($68 for eight reports, no supplements). In each case, the ARIS listing includes the name and telephone number of the grant administrator. All three reports including supplements can be secured for $240 a year. In addition, ARIS now runs a service called AIDS (Aris Information Dissemination Service), a 24-hour-a-day recorded hotline that subscribers can call for updates of information from all sources. Researchers can subscribe to the telephone service separately for $35 a year.

All the above are available from Academic Research Information System, Pacific Medical Center, 2330 Clay Street, Suite 205, San Francisco, CA 94115, (415) 922-9080.

☐ *College and University Reports.* This two-volume loose-leaf system with weekly supplements is designed primarily for use by fundraisers in higher education. It covers institutional, teacher and student programs, reports on federally-sponsored research and includes a federal agency directory. (It also covers related matters such as government procurement, tax questions, application of federal laws, Congressional actions affecting higher education and new laws and regulations.)

The service costs $680 a year, $1,240 for two years from Commerce Clearinghouse, Inc., 4025 West Peterson Avenue, Chicago, IL 60646, (312) 583-8500.

☐ *Federal Grants and Contracts Weekly.* This newsletter publishes all newly-announced requests for proposals (RFPs) from the government's complicated *Commerce Business Daily,* newly-announced federal grants from various sources, regulations that affect grant-seeking groups, news of the federal grants and contracts world and agency profiles.

The service costs $114 a year from Capitol Publications, Inc., 2430 Pennsylvania Avenue, N.W., Washington, DC 20037.

☐ *Federal Notes.* Despite its title, this 22-times-a-year newsletter covers not only the full range of RFPs, contracts and general grant programs, but those of quasi-governmental and independent scholarly and research organizations as well. Filing deadlines are prominently displayed. The publisher also offers grant consultation and proposal-writing workshops.

Federal Notes costs $72 a year, $135 for two years from Federal Development Associates, P.O. Box 986, Saratoga, CA 95070, (408) 354-4557.

☐ *FRAS News Notes.* Published by the Federal Resources Advisory Service, its target audience is college and university development directors. This monthly scans Department of Education, National Endowment for the Arts, National Endowment for the Humanities, National Institutes of Health and National Science Foundation programs.

FRAS News Notes is available from Federal Resources Advisory Service, 1818 R Street, N.W., Washington, DC 20009, (202) 387-3760.

☐ *The Grantsmanship Center.* This Los Angeles organization provides a broad range of grant resources. Its *Grantsmanship Center News* is the largest publication of its kind—80,000 subscribers. Long features, available as reprints, include useful articles on every aspect of fundraising, government administration, tax and accounting problems, prospect research, proposal writing and negotiation and business giving-patterns. Four special reprints identify grant resources in the field of aging, rehabilitation, arts and humanities and mental health services. The Center also conducts training seminars, small-enrollment, five-day workshops based on the Center's popular grant-writing system.

Publications list or subscriptions to *Grantsmanship Center News* ($20 a year, $36 for two years, $50 for three years; six issues a year) from The Grantsmanship Center, 1031 South Grand Avenue, Los Angeles, CA 90015.

☐ *The Research Monitor.* A weekly news service organized to be maintained as a reference work, covering all federal extramural (outside-of-government) funding programs. Each program gets its own two-page profile, and roughly 500 are covered in the current master volume. New profile updates are published weekly, plus a newsletter that also carries news on solicitations from all sources. Loose-leaf format. For new subscribers, $550 brings the complete current volume plus a year's service of updates and news. Renewal cost thereafter, $45 a year. A volume of the profiles only: $275. Newsletter only: $150 a year.

   The above are available from the National Information Service, 1754 Church Street, N.W., Washington, DC 20036, (202) 234-6630.

☐ *Taft Foundation Reporter.* This 397-page collection of research from one of America's leading fundraising counselors costs $220. The company also consults on grant programs and every aspect of raising money for nonprofit projects. (One of their ideas was *Smithsonian Magazine*, a giant financial shot-in-the-arm for "America's attic.")

   Send for information about their services to: Taft Corporation, 1000 Vermont Avenue, N.W., Washington, DC 20005.

☐ *Washington International Arts Letter.* This for-profit organization culls all sources for grants available in the world of arts, much as do the scientific and technical services listed above. The *Washington International Arts Letter* costs $16 a year for individuals, $32 for institutions. Two other publications, edited by the *Letter*'s Daniel Millsaps, categorize aid as follows: *National Directory of Arts Support by Private Foundations.* 1977. 264 pages. $75. *National Directory of Grants and Aid to Individuals in the Arts,* 4th edition. 1980. 231 pages. $15.95.

   These publications are available from: Washington International Arts Letter, Box 9005, Washington, DC 20003.

☐ *IRS and state tax records.* Foundations must report each year to the IRS, revealing their assets, who got grants for how much, changes in structure and leadership, and so on. In some states, they must file similar reports with the tax board, treasurer, corporations department, Secretary of State or Attorney General. Librarians at one of your state's special foundation research collections will know about the local reports, and may have them on file. Although the IRS reports aren't filed until May for the year before, they are the ultimate resource for determining how a federally-recognized foundation is spending its money. IRS Form 990-AR is the foundation's annual report following standards decreed by the government; Form 990-PF is how private foundations certify compliance with tax laws. Aside from special collections, there are two other ways to look at these records without cost:

- The IRS, through certain regional field offices, will order up an entire state's most recent Forms 990, which are stored on computer cards with microfilm inserts, called aperture cards. You can scan the reports at the IRS office and order copies made from them, paying only for the copies you need.

- Each foundation is required by law to maintain copies of its most recent Forms 990 at its principal office and to show them to you upon request. In the case of many small private foundations, you'll be dealing with a legal firm or a bank's trust department, but approach the task optimistically and report any refusal on the foundation's part to the IRS.

☐ *Corporate grants: starting points.* Corporate giving, both directly and through company foundations, surpassed private foundation spending for the first time in 1979, but the research materials available in this field are far thinner. The Foundation Center is expanding its research in this category, which it has identified as the only class of foundation to have stayed ahead of inflation.

☐ *Corporate Foundation Profiles* analyzes over 200 of the biggest company foundations—those that give more than $100,000 a year or have assets of more than $1 million. The listings reveal address, phone number, officers and staff names, information about the parent company, current financial data (including grant ranges), publications issued by each, policy statements, grant lists and analysis by category. $50 from The Foundation Center, 888 Seventh Avenue, New York, NY 10106.

☐ The Washington International Arts Letter publishes a survey of corporate giving in its special field: *National Directory of Arts Support by Business Corporations.* 1979. 221 pages. $65 from Washington International Arts Letter, P.O. Box 9005, Washington, DC 20003.

☐ The American Council for the Arts publishes *A Guide to Corporate Giving in the Arts.* 1978. 403 pages. $13.75 from the American Council for the Arts, 870 Seventh Avenue, New York, NY 10018.

☐ The Business Committee for the Arts provides a public-relations-style liaison between grant-seekers and corporate givers. Its 47-page roster of past largesse is *5,123 Examples of How BCA Companies Supported the Arts in '78 and '79.* Free from Business Committee for the Arts, 1500 Broadway, New York, NY 10036.

☐ The Human Resources Network of Philadelphia produced two massive works in the mid-70s. *The User's Guide to Funding Resources* covers all areas of grants, and is a valuable reference work, still available from the Network for $39.95. But larger, and unique, is its *Handbook of Corporate Social Responsibility: Profiles of Involvement,* which corporations as well as grant-seekers pay attention to. It's 629 pages of dense facts, kept in print by Chilton at $42. Order from Human Resources Network, 2010 Chancellor Street, Philadelphia, PA 19103.

☐ *Personal sources and networks.* People are more important than paperwork, and while personal contacts won't be able to recite numbers and addresses the printed sources contain, their eyewitness testimony about funding groups they've dealt with is important in the first stages of prospect research and indispensable later. Consider:

- Staff and board members of projects similar to your own. Although technically you may be competitors for grant money, you may find it useful to swap information.

- The financial and development officers of any institution with which you are, or have been, affiliated.

- Networks and shelter groups, that exist in many areas to share the costs of prospect research. Mentors and leaders in your field should know of them. Sometimes they're operated by . . .

- The staffs of unions and professional associations.

- Fundraising specialists in the regional office of your religious organization. Ask your pastor, priest or rabbi to help you open the door.

- The staffs of public interest law and accounting firms that now exist in many cities. They may have been intimately involved in chores for local foundations and other nonprofit sources. You may be able to determine their existence with the help of your local Bar Association or Society of Certified Public Accountants.

- Bankers and lawyers. The ones you can reach directly or through an intermediary, but specifically lawyers who prepare trusts and estates and bankers who work in the trust department. They are, by profession, experts on local foundations. If you're a member of a minority community served by a special-interest bank, the trust department of that bank should be especially helpful.

☐ *Three obvious, but sometimes overlooked sources:*

- Bulletin boards. Most institutions of any size that receive non-profit funding get announcements of open programs for posting, and many actually post them.

- Acknowledgments. Even your biggest local competitor for the same dollar is likely to thank its contributors in its annual report, newsletter, theatrical program, exhibit catalog or whatever it publishes. Similarly, most scholarly and scientific papers funded by grants acknowledge the donor upon publication, sometimes in the "Notes to Contributors" section of the journal.

- The Yellow Pages. Mother Bell's designation is "Foundations-Educational, Philanthropic, Research, etc." Some of the foundations listed there will be nonprofit organizations that don't make grants. But others are the real thing, and the value of the Yellow Pages listing is its signal to you that the foundation has an office, phone number and at least one full-time staff member—which most foundations don't.

Analyzing your prospects

With your prospect sheets in hand, it's time to decide the potential value to you of each source and to assign a specific target figure that you're going to ask for.

The prospect analysis sheet breaks roughly into thirds, along the lines of the three basic steps in research:

- The information you have gotten from standard printed sources, such as directories, newsletters and library files. (The top third of the form.)

- The information you will develop through direct contact with the funding source. (The program summary, deadlines, and grant analysis sections of the form.)

- The listing and assignment of tasks you'll share with colleagues, board members, informal sponsors, mentors, and so on—those upon whom you rely for both information and action. (The outside connections lines, and the target figure you decide upon.)

If you run out of space on the form, simply number and add as many additional pages as you need. It's also a good idea to keep a record of correspondence, calls and any other contacts by simply listing them in chronological order on the back of the form. We've already covered the basic research, so let's examine the direct contacts and how you work with your helpers.

FIRST CONTACTS WITH THE FUNDING SOURCE

The distance, size and nature of the source dictates the nature of first contact. It can be a personal visit, a letter or a telephone call. The information you're seeking is the same:

- Verify data already on the sheet: basic stuff like name, address, phone number and so on.

- Ask for a copy of the funding body's annual report, if any, together with any printed program summary and any materials that have been designed specifically to help applicants.

- Get the names and telephone extension numbers of the persons who actually will read your proposal and steer it through the internal decision-making machinery.

You should be prepared to tell the prospect who you are and what your project is in your first letter or conversation. A first letter should request a specific date and time for a personal meeting or a telephone conversation. In the case of small foundations administered by banks, law firms and business boards, you may be dealing with an administrative secretary or assistant whose role *vis à vis* the foundation is to contain the paperwork and the trouble it causes. Persevere. Such minor functionaries, if treated with everyday courtesy and patience, can become valuable advocates for your project. The further information you will need to develop will vary, according to whether you're applying as an individual or for an institution, to a foundation or corporate program or to the government. For this reason, use the questions below to tailor the "grant analysis" section of your prospect sheet to match your project as closely as possible. Place checkmarks alongside the questions that apply to your project. In using the form and the questions, be informal and conversational. An interrogation by checklist is a bad first impression.

Checklist: questions that fill out the picture

☐ Do you make grants to individuals, to organizations, to administering institutions? (As applicable to your case—a case you may want to change by adopting formal shelter or incorporating, if research suggests it.)

☐ Are your grants restricted to tax-deductible organizations?

☐ Do you restrict your gifts to tax-deductible organizations to those in the higher (or "50-percent") category of deductibility: public charities?

☐ What about the scale of your gifts—the biggest, the smallest and the average for the past couple of funding periods?

☐ Do you require any outside approvals before accepting a proposal? (In private and corporate foundations: the approval of a local advisory or shelter organization in your field of endeavor. In government programs: approval by local or state offices that oversee and rank applications for funds in their field.)

☐ What's the maximum share of a project's total cost that you feel comfortable about funding?

☐ Do you look for government participation in the budget, or do you prefer projects that are privately funded?

☐ Do you restrict your gifts to one-time grants, or are there certain recipients you're willing to work with on a long-term basis?

☐ Are you willing to fund projects that require one-time capital outlays for buildings, equipment and so on, or do you tend to restrict your grants to operational funding?

☐ Are you willing to fund projects that involve hiring staff members who are exclusively committed to that project?

☐ Do you place any limit on how much of the grant can be expended on salaries, or on the size of salaries under the grant?

☐ What limits, if any, do you place on the amount of institutional overhead ("indirect costs") included in our budget?

☐ Do you initiate, or help match, challenge or matching grants? If so, what ratios do you follow, how long do we have to make the match and what restrictions, if any, do you place on the source of matching funds?

☐ Do you have any special requirements—or informal policies that have the same weight—we should keep in mind when applying to you?

☐ Will you be willing to meet with us before your deadline and discuss how closely what we're proposing meets your idea of a good project?

☐ Can you give us an idea of where projects like ours now rank in your grant pattern?

☐ Can you tell us who is our competition for a project like this and what you like about their proposal?

USING HELPERS

The final step of prospect research involves reaching out to the directors, advisors, mentors or colleagues who are helping you in your quest—

specifically, those with direct knowledge about the target prospects. This technique of shared work is especially useful in the case of small organizations going after local corporate or foundation funds as all or part of their budget. The best way to do the job is in meetings, or a series of them, in which one source's recollections inspire those of others. Associates with a formal or informal link to the prospect, such as a board position, should be listed in the "outside connections" spaces. Their in-person role in the direct solicitation process is described ahead, but for now, it's intelligence-gathering through meetings or conversations with insiders. These need not necessarily be foundation staff or board members. Accountants, lawyers, social acquaintances or previous recipients are good sources for them to turn to—the school of "pilot fish" who circle every large body of money.

ASSIGNING THE GOAL

This is it. In print, in person, inside, outside, you've learned everything possible about your likeliest prospects. Based on your needs and their giving pattern, assign each a dollar figure you're seeking, whatever share of the budget it represents. This is the final step of research.

The Case Statement
(and Its Supporting Evidence)

The general idea

The case statement is the heart of the grant proposal—a very few pages that say in plain and effective language what you intend to do and why the people you're addressing should give you the money.

First-time grant applicants can be obsessive about determining the magic format for their proposal. There is none—no way of choosing and arranging words that will drive prospective givers mad with generosity.

Instead, you must create or adapt a form you feel comfortable with—one that reflects your way of expressing yourself but, more importantly, one that logically presents all the vital data the proposal *must* include:

- The basic premise—the problem or challenge and your approach and method for meeting it.

- The setting of the project, meaning its place in a body of ongoing work and, if appropriate, its institutional framework.

- The people involved, whether it's simply you or a big team. Why are they qualified to do this job well?

- The costs of the proposed project and how the source's contribution will fit into the total budget picture.

Some aspects of the budget, and of the matters that I categorize as "shelter and reassurance," are covered in the next chapter, but the guts of your proposal lie in the four elements listed above. Your job is to satisfy your readers' questions about these matters before they arise.

The case statement, or project narrative, is a job of reporting. The facts have to stand up and fight for themselves. Adjectives and emotions must be ruthlessly barred. Your job is to stand back and look at the project through the eyes of an outsider, someone who lacks the passionate self-interest you naturally feel about what you're setting out to do.

In order to write the case statement, you need to know all of the supporting evidence such as methodology and budgeting, and an early draft may help focus your planning. Creating this prose centerpiece of the proposal becomes a moment of truth, because if you find yourself unable to explain matters in the direct and concise fashion preached here, something is very likely wrong with the project itself. Go back to the four questions at the beginning of the Handbook section and ask yourself what's missing.

You should go to work on the case statement and the other written parts of the proposal at the same time you begin your basic search for prospects. Each job helps the other. What your research reveals will help you shape the final proposal to match real-world giving patterns, and the draft case statement will help you explain yourself to others at this stage of the game.

Proposal format

You should prepare a proposal whose form closely relates to and enhances your project design. Certain government programs require you to use forms, but aside from pages on budgeting and legal requirements, on which it's obvious you should fill out each line, you often can use basic materials from your general proposal, breaking them up into exhibits or attachments you refer to in the appropriate blank.

The key elements of the finished proposal should include:

• A cover letter, or letter of transmittal.

- A title page that gives:

  - Your name, or that of your group.

  - The proposal or project title. ("Proposal for an Inner-City Debt Counseling Service" or "Proposal for a Mid-Career Travel and Research Sabbatical.")

  - The name of the funding body you're applying to, and the date. ("Submitted to the Waldo C. Buckner Foundation, October 1, 1981.")

- A summary introduction that says, in just a few paragraphs, who you are, what you propose to do, how and why. In proposals for formal research this is the *abstract*, which will be developed in the body of your text. In all cases, this brief introduction is an essential element.

- Additional paragraphs or sections, titled if they are lengthy, that set forth:

  - The problem or challenge you're trying to meet with your project, together with *succinct* data that support your view of the problem.

  - The unique qualifications that make you or your group capable of carrying out the project.

  - The method, work-plan or research methodology you intend to follow in doing so, including a summarized timetable of project events.

  - The people involved in the work, described by a table of organization, brief statements of their qualifications, or both. In the case of individual applicants, this is where you summarize your life and work experiences leading up to the application and refer the proposal reader to work samples, such as abstracts or copies of publications, slides of artwork, reviews of performances, and so on. Some applicants tend to swamp their proposal readers with scrapbooks only a mother could love (or keep). Instead, you should reduce such exhibits to 8½ × 11 sheets of paper through reduction photocopying and limit special exhibits, such as slides, to a single, notebook-sized plastic slide storage sheet.

- A brief statement of your plans for self-evaluation or for evaluation by the funding group.

- The one-page budget, described later in this chapter.

- Supplementary exhibits, such as legal papers and testimonials, that fall under the heading of shelter, incorporation and association, and which are described in detail in the following chapter.

Some grant counselors answer beginners' nervousness about precise formats by prescribing one. But there are only so many counselors and guides, and following a copied-out format diminishes the unique qualities of your proposal, turning it into a duplicate of all the others that follow the same formula. What you should do, instead, is circle or underline the elements above that belong in your proposal and include them in that order, giving your reader enough headings and subheads (simply use capitals or underlining) and enough white space for easy reading. The proposal must be typewritten, preferably on an electric typewriter, and should be double-spaced.

The finished items should be submitted as a stack of 8½ × 11 sheets held together with a paper clip or clamp. Elaborate bindings and presentation folders not only betray amateurism, but are a nuisance. (You should expect that your reader will want to duplicate certain pages of the proposal for internal review, and loose-leaf or bound formats only get in the way.)

Far, far more important than how the proposal looks is how well it's written.

Crash course:
eight guidelines to writing for proposal writers

BE A REPORTER

Meaning, set out the facts in a manner that makes the conclusions draw themselves. You should report exactly the way your high school journalism teacher taught: the five w's and the h. Who, what, where, when, why. The "h" stands for how, and in the world of grants, you need another "h" for how *much* (it is all going to cost).

This doesn't mean you have to recite the five w's in the order cub reporters memorize them—simply make sure you get them all in. To see how, take a blank sheet of paper, turn it sideways, list the five w's and the two h's across the top and start a list of the facts you're including:

- Who? You, your institution or the *ad hoc* project team inside that institution or organization.

- What? A project to discover, create, correct, identify, add to the body of knowledge about, enable, make available, cure, entertain, save, stamp out. Search for the verb at the heart of the process and use it in its strongest forms.

- Where? In a community where everyone agrees it's one of the biggest problems. Before an audience of people who never have had a chance to see this on stage. In a laboratory uniquely equipped for research into this question. At our legal clinic, which has a successful, ten-year history of managing similar programs. Telling the *where* of your story isn't a matter of naming the right address, but of putting your project into the context of the problem and/or similar, successful work in the same direction.

- When? Another chance to put your proposal into *context*. Remember: grant readers frown at ideas that stand alone and give the impression of having been invented for purposes of getting the money. Your project should have a reasonable time frame that can be explained in a few sentences, breaking the work down into stages and offering deadlines that you (and your funding groups) can use to check progress. If you're describing an ongoing project, explain why you need the money you're asking for at this particular stage of the work.

- Why? Because there's a specific need, and this project is designed to answer it. Show the need as vividly and convincingly as the facts allow.

- *How?* Tell how the program you've devised answers that specific need in the most direct and appropriate fashion. The *why* and the *how* are the heart of the heart of your grant, and if either side of this essential equation is weak or missing, the givers will turn to stronger proposals.

- How much? You explain yourself a page or two later with a budget, a piece of paper where all the words are married to numbers. Prefaces, postscripts and footnotes are out. If it won't fit on one page, it's too detailed. Remember, if corporations that handle billions of dollars a year can tell the story on a single sheet of paper, so can you. A budget shows money moving through time, and the time span you show should match the period in which you'll be spending the money you seek. The budget also will show all sources of revenue, including the part your prospective donors would play. All four factors of the cash element—income, sources, expenses and time—are worth a mention in the opening paragraphs of the case statement, but the budget page is the page that counts, and it rates a section of its own later in this chapter.

Now, if you've conducted the exercise of listing the essential facts under columns on a sheet of paper—the five w's and the two h's—you may be put off by the notion of assembling all these items into a piece of prose that reads as if it were written by a human being, not a computer. Here's where another bit of high school journalism wisdom comes into play.

THE INVERTED PYRAMID

This simply means that you put the most important stuff at the top and the less important stuff at the bottom. It's how wire services write the news; today's paper is full of examples. It's a technique invented because the wire service writer is writing for hundreds of papers, including some that won't have enough room for the whole story. This way, the story still makes sense if it gets cut off from the bottom. In the same way, *your* story will make sense to the prospective givers (or their colleagues) who are so flooded by applications and pressed for time that they can't, or don't, read to the end. For that reason, you need to summarize as many of the facts as possible in your opening lines—the lead, in newspaper talk—and then, in the remainder of your brief narrative, develop them in order of diminishing importance.

USE PLAIN ENGLISH

The best way to do this is to write the way you talk. The way you *really* talk—not how you think you'd speak before an audience of bigwigs considering your grant. And the best way to test whether you're doing this is to read aloud what you've written. Contractions ("you'd" for "you would," "you've" for "you have") are okay and so are words like "okay." Also, for that matter, occasional sentences without verbs, such as this one.)

Another simple way to see whether your writing is on the right track is to read it through and ask yourself whether a foreigner with a limited grasp of English could easily follow what you've set down. If not, translate for this imaginary visitor. If you can't say it simply, you probably don't have much to say (or much worth reading).

Novice grant writers—and even some of the veterans—have a tendency to deck out their ideas with words and phrases that are intended to make things sound more official, scientific, complicated, certain, important or learned than they really are. English is a living language, which means that new words and phrases and new ways of using old ones are constantly cropping up and being tested, but a grant application is a lousy place to launch them. The enemy is jargon, which the dictionary defines as both "nonsensical, incoherent, or meaningless utterance" and "the specialized or technical language of a trade, profession or class." In the world of grants, earnest proposal writers often pack their prose with examples of the second definition, insider talk, and wind up with examples of the first sort, gibberish.

Of course, if you're writing about a scientific or highly technical project, the language of your specialty is appropriate. You don't have to sound like a script for *Sesame Street* when you know that the proposal reader shares much of your knowledge about your field of specialization and will recognize terms you use because they're precise and effective.

But all too often, these insider-words become a kind of code that, consciously or not, has the effect of barricading reader and writer against the world of those who don't understand them, who aren't in the know. Jargon, in grant proposals, is a lame tactic for sucking up to your imaginary reader by shaping your thoughts into the form you think is *expected* of you instead of expressing yourself clearly. In some cases, proposals are reviewed by lay persons who are irritated by undue reliance on insider-talk and may very well throw their support behind a proposal they can understand. (Senator Proxmire's rather successful vendetta against government funding of pure scientific research relies for its success upon the inherent humor, to lay readers, of technical forms of expression.)

Some grant consultants actually preach effective use of jargon and buzzwords, and in certain fields, such as education and the social sciences—areas where the connection between everyday life and speech and the specialty itself seems both necessary and desirable—the game is very nearly over: the people involved really are *talking* this way.

William and Mary Morris, a husband-and-wife team of word experts, edit the *Harper Dictionary of Contemporary Usage*, a 600-plus-page collection of articles about problem words, written with the help of 136 experts on the language. William Morris is the editor-in-chief of *The American Heritage Dictionary of the English Language*, the best American dictionary in print. The Morrises have identified dozens of examples of "vogue words" infiltrating the language, words like *benchmark, overview, phase in* (and *phase out), ongoing, in depth, interface, parameter, peer group, synergy* and *synergistic.* The Morrises write optimistically that these words are headed for "the limbo reserved for the vogue words of yesteryear," and cite "priority" as an example of a dead buzzword. (Obviously, their reading priorities don't include many grant proposals.) And new horrors, like "wellness," are creeping in all the time. Werner Erhard, the motel-ballroom guru of est, is waging war on innocent conjunctions like "but," while trying to launch new locutions such as "at the effect of" to describe something or someone influenced by something or someone else. (A whole dictionary full of Erhard's linguistic lunacy has been making the rounds of publishers for years, and his followers already talk this way.)

Defenders of words like "interface" and "parameter" argue that no other single word will do the job as well and, besides, these days only an idiot would fail to understand them. Maybe so, but their use betrays a tone-deafness about the language and a certain misunderstanding about what language is—a system of symbols in which the broadest possible understanding is a virtue. You have to decide for yourself whether to reach out to the widest audience possible or to barricade yourself against the world of the unwashed by invoking the code of the insiders. My preference is plain and my advice is to be mindful of proposal readers who think as I do, who read "at this point in time" when "right now" is correct and throw your proposal on the reject stack.

The Bible of plain English is *The Elements of Style*, a student writing handbook by Professor William Strunk of Cornell, revised and updated by his student E. B. White, who followed the advice it contained and became America's leading essayist of the 20th century, a master of clarity and concision.

Strunk and White's advice about active verb forms versus passive ones, about the nature of the paragraph and the virtues of pacing—this is grade-A stuff, the perfect example of how much true wisdom can be crammed into a very small book.

To see the advice in action, you might do as many professional writers do and read a few pages of really good English before sitting down to write your own. Anything by White, including his children's books like *Charlotte's Web*, would be a good choice, and so would anything by Mark Twain, Winston Churchill or Kurt Vonnegut, Jr.

WRITE TO A SPECIFIC READER

This doesn't necessarily mean the decision-maker whose name and tastes may, as a result of good prospect research, be an open book to you. This old rule of writers and writing teachers simply means that you have a certain, real-life human being in mind, someone you know well enough to imagine them stopping as they read and asking you "What does this mean?" or saying, "If you don't mind my advice, I think the whole second part was pretty dense and dull." My imaginary reader is an old friend named Bill who has been an actor, rock musician, novelist, advertising man and screenwriter. I didn't pick him as imaginary reader because of his job qualifications, but because he represents an intelligent person who may be unfamiliar with the technical subjects I sometimes write about. It doesn't matter to me whether Bill actually bothers to read this book or anything else I've written with him in mind. It's just that I know him so well I can imagine him saying, in one of the accents left over from his acting days, "I say, old man, I think you got a bit carried away with your attack on jargon." (And I can imagine his wife, Carol, arguing that it displayed a vital element in writing: passion.)

BE PASSIONATE, BE COOL

Passion and distance are the *yin* and *yang* of writing, and controlling the tension between them is the writer's essential art. This control is what let Shakespeare cover the stage with corpses at the end of the play, while writing iambic pentameter lines that people still quote four hundred years later.

You don't have to be Shakespeare to do it. The anonymous reporters who wrote about the assassinations of the Kennedy brothers and Martin Luther King, and the aftermath of those events, managed to convey the passion contained in the events without straying from the plain-English-please rules of their form.

Why passion?

I once asked a very wise philanthropist, a giver on the grand scale, what he looked for in a proposal. "Passion," he said. "And it's the same in my business. I tend to trust people who are *passionate* about what they do."

Being a passionate person doesn't mean wearing your feelings on your sleeve, or slopping adjectives and asides all over your grant proposal. It means feeling so intensely about your project that the depth of your feeling is reflected in the care you've taken in designing and describing it. If it's there, it shows.

Sometimes it shows too much. Grant writers need a touch of coolness about their prose to temper their passionate concern. If you're too demonstrative and emotional in your prose, you're pegged as an amateur. In seeking grants in areas of social need, you may be sorely tempted to play the heartstrings, to lapse into poster-child case histories about the orphan who needs your day-care center because her blind grandmother goes to work at dawn and returns after dark. Remember: problem/solution. If your writing shows that you understand the problem so well you can state it simply, and that your solution is both logical and the product of your intelligent and passionate concern, you're writing a first-rate proposal.

The ultimate no-no in a proposal is the "Where-would-I-be-without-you?" syndrome, in which you're so foolish as to tell the reader you can't do the job without his help. As true as that may be, revealing it betrays the thinness of your general effort to get money and puts the would-be giver in an uncomfortable and unwanted role. This is the kind of information best conveyed, if at all, during direct conversation, through a remark such as, "Frankly, if you and the feds don't come through, we may have to throw in the towel." Unsought declarations of dependence are the stuff of song lyrics, not grant proposals. Making the point at all is questionable, making it in writing is a potentially fatal error, and pressing it can infuriate a prospect and close a door to you forever.

GET PERSONAL

When I was very small, a family friend named Rudolf Flesch gave me a copy of a book he had written called *The Art of Readable Writing*. You can still find it in libraries, and it's interesting, because Dr. Flesch used statistics to dismantle writing that worked and figure out what made it tick. A couple of his prescriptions are obvious: shorter words and shorter sentences. But one of his ideas is an important observation, and it's stuck with me since I first read it as a child. The more personal the prose, the more readable and effective. That is, the more real-life characters, (like me and Dr. Flesch, in this paragraph), the more pronouns, the better.

First person prose where the author is on-stage, starring as "I," is okay for a book like this with its informal tone, and in the relatively narrow world of grants to individuals, especially in the arts. But it's usually ruled out, and so is second person writing, where "you" become the subject of the sentence, an exercise in mind-reading that is fast-wearying.

But first person *plural*—we, us—that's something else. If your proposal is about a team project, use "we" and "us," instead of going to the trouble of depersonalizing your prose. "Him," "her," "they"—all of them, as Dr. Flesch's magic numbers proved, make readers sit up and pay more attention.

Pronouns pay off.

SHOW MOMENTUM

Give your writing about your project a sense that things are underway, that you're building on the past and have the future clearly in mind. The idea is to make your project stand out as part of a continuing effort, a logical extension of the experience that will contribute to this new venture's success. Momentum—a word on loan to the language from physics—describes this sense perfectly.

What grant readers don't want to see (or *fund*) are projects that look as though they were dreamed up for the purpose of getting the money—ideas that don't feel real on paper because, in fact, they're not. Your project needs a past as well as a future, and so you're obliged to convey this sense of work-in-motion, while taking care not to waste your reader's time (and your limited space) with a potentially boring exhibition of previous trophies and achievements.

USE GUINEA PIGS

Advertising agencies, especially the ones that supervise million-dollar budgets, have a process they call copy testing, a formal method for "running it up the flagpole to see if anyone salutes." Without resorting to their elaborate questionnaires, you should follow the same procedure with your case statement. Show your work to friends and colleagues you trust and ask for their reactions. (One good way to see whether the writing works is to watch them read it. Frowns, squints and fingers scanning lines often mean clumsy or puzzling construction.)

Some of your test-readers may have ideas for beautifying your prose—ideas it may be just as well to ignore. The main value of these guinea pigs is to discover if you left anything out, if a key transition doesn't work, if the case statement includes any sentences that have to be read twice to make sense. Make it clear in advance that you won't be embarrassed by what they say, and keep the bargain. Your case statement is working prose, not lyric poetry. If the consensus is to make changes, make them.

Supporting evidence: people pages

Curriculum vitae, or "CV," as you'll often hear it called, is Latin for "the story of your life," or, to be precise, "the course of one's life." If you're applying for a grant as an individual, your proposal should include a CV. If you're seeking money for a bigger project, it's an excellent idea to prepare brief résumés of key people involved in the undertaking. Another way of handling this aspect of the multi-person project is to prepare a "team biography" that emphasizes your team members' study and work experiences in your field of endeavor.

The grant reader isn't interested in learning that you were Posture Princess in the fifth grade, or how many merit badges you earned in Scouts. The information included should have a direct bearing on the project at hand, showing the sweep of personal history that has led you to the point of asking for the money.

Résumés or CVs can move forward or backward in time, ending or starting with the present, and some people like to emphasize the particular role they played as the first line of each entry, such as: "Development Director, Buckner Museum of Black-Velvet Painting, Buckner TX, 1977–79." Others list the dates first, which gives the finished product an inexorable, march-of-time air and emphasizes any gaps of joblessness or "self-employment."

For clarity, you can break the CV into little sections, such as "education," "professional experience," "honors and awards," and "publications" (or "performances," "exhibits" . . . whatever applies in your case.)

Unless you've lived an especially long, rich and full life—or if you're an individual applicant in whose case an extremely thorough picture of your work is appropriate—you should try to throw away everything that won't fit onto a single page.

The same is true of the final, vital element of the grant proposal—your budget.

Supporting evidence: the budget

To the money managers reading it, your budget page is perhaps the most concrete element of your proposal. It's the nitty-gritty, the place where they can see at a glance how much money you want from them and how it fits into your program.

Because government grant applications are designed to handle huge scale programs, as well as small ones, their budget pages are correspondingly intricate. If you cannot understand them, you should go to someone in the funding agency for help. (Perhaps the most puzzling aspect of these government budget forms is something called "indirect costs," which amounts to the value of the shelter and services offered by the group initiating and managing, or simply overseeing, the project. Indirect costs count as matching funds in some programs, and some proposal writers treat them as marvelously malleable funny-money. Be careful.)

But if, as will usually be the case, you're applying to a foundation or a corporate program, a budget like the one in Figure 2 (see Appendix Three) will do the job. Let's go through the form, checking off what's necessary in your case.

Checklist: budget essentials

☐ *Say what it is at the top.* The budget for *what.* And say who the applying group (or individual) is. *Don't* mark the budget as "submitted to," naming the prospect; it gives the impression that you ran up this budget especially for them, a bad mistake.

☐ *Spending on the left, getting on the right.* The material on the left side of the budget page shows where and how you're spending the money. The columns at the right show, in order, the amount of each item's cost you expect from the funding source; the money for that cost already raised, firmly expected or arranged for as overhead, indirect costs or grants-in-kind; and finally, at right, the total cost for each item. Reading vertically, you can find category subtotals and totals.

☐ *Cluster by category.* Most budgets break neatly down into the three categories in the example: salaries, services and one-time start-up (or capital) costs. Let's examine each.

   ☐ *Salaries.* In the case of a grant to an individual, this section could be headed, instead, "living expenses," and provide detail on use of money for a sabbatical year. Or in the case of a sheltered research grant, the money for salary sought should be described in terms of a fraction, or percentage, of your total salary. (The funding source's contribution replaces your institution's full support for a certain part of your time, freeing you for the work.) Salaries demonstrated as grants-in-kind can represent the loan of full- or part-time workers by the group that is parent to the project. In the example, on the line for the half-time debt counselors, the licensed social workers, the $16,600 figure for persons at different wage levels was achieved by working backward from the total salary for the three, working half-time. For some projects you may need to add a line to this section covering *benefits*, which includes employer's insurance contributions, state unemployment and disability fund payments, and so on.

☐ *Services*, easily defined as anything that isn't salaries and benefits and doesn't result in the acquisition of permanent, capital assets (like buildings and typewriters). This cluster of items may include rent, telephones, office machine rental, insurance (other than employee-related premiums), office supplies, art materials, film stock, audiotape and videotape, and so on . . . things you rent, that other people do for you or that get used up. Contingencies, calculated here at a reasonable 15 percent of the services subtotal, belong in every budget. It's something funding sources expect you to include, but don't want to pay for. (Because around many projects, it's the slush fund.) At 15 percent, it's also a prudent hedge against inflation as well as unexpectedly high costs in a particular category.

☐ *One-time costs.* Some sources pay them and others shy away. All are interested in seeing them, because, in the case of money that is restricted to operations, they help prove there's something to operate. This category may be totally missing from academic research projects, scientific studies and individual grants to fine artists, composers or writers.

☐ *Keep it clean and simple.* Certain government grants require calculations to the penny, but for most funding sources, the rounded-off form adopted here is okay. You can round off at fives, tens, the next-highest fifty, or whatever; simply be consistent. You'll notice that the sample budget doesn't throw in ugly dotted lines to lead the reader's eye to the figures, nor, except for organizational names, does it use upper case, or capital, letters. The lower case style is far easier to read than the one that confers capitals upon unworthy nouns, such as "Postage."

☐ *Keep it honest.* Sooner or later, you'll hear about the "fudge factor"—the budget line, or lines, whose total cost has been inflated a bit to lubricate the functioning of the eventual project. All funding sources know that your follow-up report to them will not match to the penny the original budget you submit. Getting money back is pure fiction. But inflating your budget is a tricky stunt with readers who are quite familiar with the costs involved, and it cuts into your competitive edge. Follow-up reports, which may require formal accounting, and dread on-site inspections of project and books can reveal these deceptions and hurt you permanently. The fat line for travel, the staff car, the inflated contingency figure—these are screaming sirens and blinking red stoplights to the knowledgeable money-manager who'll read your proposal. The grants game is one game where it really pays to be holier than God.

Shelter, Association and Incorporation

The psychological basis of continuing success in getting grants is an ability to overcome the givers' fear of the unknown. The money managers know that proposals that look good on paper can fail because the people behind the project lack experience or the whole project lacks the correct institutional or organizational framework. The decision-makers prefer known quantities. Familiarity breeds grants.

Because of these worries, many funding sources have developed formal and informal ways of protecting themselves against proposals that stand in splendid, but bothersome, isolation. Among them:

- Restricting grants to tax-exempt organizations recognized by the IRS.

- Restricting grants to large and familiar institutions that dispense the funds, such as research grants, to independent contractors who assume a quasi-employee status.

- Restricting application to groups that have existed without the funding source's aid for a given period of time, such as two or three years.

- Accepting only those applications cleared or checked and ranked by those local authorities who by law or practice are given a hand in the decision-making process.

Even in the case of individual applicants, the same forces are at work—a need for proposal pages that supply a category of information I call *reassurance*. In the case of individuals, the answer is shelter. For grant-seeking organizations, the choices are broader, and the most intelligent solution generally is to legally qualify as a tax-exempt association or corporation.

Unless your prospect research has revealed a very broad selection of potential funding sources willing to underwrite your work as an individual or unincorporated group, you should consider upgrading your "reassurance status."

The work involved in incorporation and securing tax-exemption looks rather daunting, but it is possible even without a lawyer's help. However, it *is* time-consuming because of the slow pace at which bureaucracies operate, so if the earliest stages of prospect research suggest this step, waste no time in getting and filing the papers. This task may become what planners call the "pacing item," the thing that, left undone, halts further progress.

In a certain sense, these reassurance tasks are like qualifying trials in sports. They cull the field. "What-if" projects are faced with the cold, hard facts of creating and maintaining an institutional reality. Few projects that exist simply to get the money will survive. The people who give the money away know this. Jumping through these particular hoops, however, will not only greatly widen your prospect list and improve your chances, it's likely that they'll make you a truly better grant recipient. There *is* a method to this particular paperwork madness.

Shelter

The simplest form of shelter is the endorsement, the statement in the form of a letter that tells the prospect that someone the funding source already knows, or knows of, has examined the proposal and finds it worthy.

In one sense, the endorsement process is a little like the Apostolic Succession, a laying-on of hands in which those who've been around for awhile certify the efforts of the newcomers as worthy of attention. If you conduct prospect research properly, you should be able to find individuals and organizations who have dealt successfully with your funding targets in the past. (Remember that not all grantees leave a good impression, so don't make the mistake of adorning your proposal with good words from people who may be on the outs with your target.) If you provide a prospect with several endorsements that reawaken memories of fruitful collaborations in the past, you've gone a long way to eradicate the fatal fear of the unknown.

Therefore, you should start seeking endorsements at the earliest stages of organizing your grant system, making sure that the file grows, letter by letter, and doesn't turn into a last-minute extra.

What makes a good endorsement?

- The status, in the eyes of the funding target, of the endorsing individual or institution.

- Evidence within the endorsement itself that the person who signed it has read and understood your proposal. (The best way to demonstrate this is for the endorser to mention one or more aspects of the proposal that make it especially attractive. Don't be embarrassed about explaining this tactic to endorsers and suggesting the angles you consider the strongest.)

- Evidence that the endorsement isn't a piece of boilerplate, throwaway charity handed you to wave wherever it will do the most good. That is to say, the endorsing letter should bear a current date and should be addressed not "to whom it may concern," but to a specific officer or executive of the funding body, or at the very least to the organization, with a "Ladies and Gentlemen" salutation. In some cases, those who are willing to endorse you may also be willing for you to draft their remarks. Take advantage of this, and write the strongest letter you can. In other cases, when an endorser has the secretarial help to make it possible, you may arrange for a master endorsement that can be retyped and readdressed at your request.

Whom should you ask for endorsements? Consider:

- Persons with a past or a current, informal connection with the organization you're seeking money from. Ask your endorser to write and send the letter to a specific insider. Include a copy of that letter in the assurance pages of your proposal.

- Mentors or peers in your own field of work, especially those whose names and reputations will be well known to the proposal readers. People to keep in mind include departmental chairmen and instructors who have taught you, your bosses and supervisors from previous stages of your career, peers whose work in your field has been recognized (making their endorsement valid) and, in general, anyone who's accessible and to whom you look up.

- "Significant others." This category of endorser is hard to define, but real. It includes those who have no formal or informal relationship with the funding body and no particular expertise in your field, but who by virtue of station or profession have established themselves as significant voices in your line of endeavor. In community service grants, for example, this might mean an important banker, lawyer or minister whose understanding of the needs of a particular community—the "problem" side of your basic grant equation—makes him or her a logical commentator and endorser. It could also include critics, reviewers and other writers who cover your field and have a broad overview, or those whose political positions—mayoral or gubernatorial advisors, for example—give them an informal overseer function as the eyes and ears of the officeholder with whom they work.

- Politicians themselves. All officeholders are asked to endorse grant proposals within their bailiwick but, being politicians, are quite cagey about what they commit to paper. Their endorsement may be especially appropriate (and multiple endorsements from politicians who are mutual opponents can be immensely impressive), but they require the utmost attention to the preceding rules about demonstrating working knowledge of the grant and speaking directly to the funding body. The way to solve the problem is through close work with the officeholder's administrative assistants, who have been instructed by the boss to keep his or her name off proposals that may later come back to haunt.

In some cases, almost all of them government grants, the legislation that created the program you're applying to gives special say-so to boards or bodies at lower levels of government. For example, the federal Department of Education may require you to consult with officials of your *state* education department, who will read your proposal and rank its importance to them. This requirement can be immensely frustrating, because in some states no plan for the use of this federal money exists at all. Thus, while the state officials are contributing essentially nothing to this line of work, they're not likely to pass up the chance to politick over it. In other cases, worthy applicants are sent to local authorities by the higher-up agency they've applied to, only to discover that the local bureaucrats have sliced up the federal pie among a throng of hungry applicants, all well known to them. Such federal legislation rarely gives the local authorities a *veto* power, but a low-ranking or withheld endorsement can still carry substantial weight against you.

These "shotgun weddings" between potentially worthy applicants and puzzled or unprepared local authorities are a challenge to the grant-seeker, and your goal should be to rehearse your case with them, to submit and argue the proposal, to indicate willingness to modify it according to proven local needs and goals and, finally, to turn these accidental overseers into ardent advocates of what you propose, willing to argue your case to the level of government above. Failing that, you should seek cordial neutrality and in any case where the local bureaucrat slams the door on you, ruling out certification, appeal that action in writing, with copies to the agency that actually is giving the money away.

Prospect research, if properly conducted, will reveal to you that everybody who gives money away is surrounded by a network of influence. Your goal in seeking endorsements is to make that network light up on your behalf like a string of Christmas-tree lights.

Association

Some grant-seekers, especially those in lines of solitary endeavor, band together to give their common cause the air of reality that funding bodies seek. *Ad hoc* projects, or individuals or teams within separate organizations who share a common goal, may find it useful to associate formally, a legal step that ratifies their seriousness but stops shy of the greater obligations involved in formal incorporation.

Later on, the participants may want to go all the way and incorporate formally. The association route is something of a trial marriage, and it permits the participants to secure federal and (if applicable) state and local tax exemption without the final bureaucratic hurdles involved in incorporating.

Who can form a nonprofit association? Any two or more persons with a common, stated goal. And the goal can be, simply and openly, to provide shared services such as bookkeeping and banking for a group of individuals who want to qualify for grants in their field.

Do you need a lawyer? Not necessarily, although a lawyer certainly can help, and calling on a public-interest law firm or legal clinic makes sense. Some low-cost group legal practices will do this kind of work. When payment is involved, ask the lawyer in advance how much it's going to cost and then decide whether to go it alone. Public-interest law firms and local law school libraries are the places to look for handbooks that sort out the special regulations that apply in your state, territory or province.

Checklist: steps to forming a nonprofit association

☐ *Decide whether you'll qualify.* The real key to qualification is acceptance as tax-exempt by the Internal Revenue Service. This process is described below in this checklist, but if you flunk the basic standards of the Internal Revenue Code, the tactic is impossible. What does the IRS want?

☐ An association "organized and operated exclusively for religious, charitable, scientific, testing for public safety, literary or educational purposes, or for the prevention of cruelty to children or animals." You'll notice that this klutzy legalese omits such recognized nonprofit groups as legal clinics, filmmakers' collectives, museums and so on. In fact, perhaps a majority of recognized nonprofit groups are omitted from specific mention. Nonetheless, when it comes to purpose, the feds' hearts are in the right place, and you'll probably find that the language above covers what you're doing. The IRS recognizes, and has code numbers, for more than 500 purposes, including "dog club" and abortion reform.

☐ The IRS reserves the right to make sure that your operations match the goals and promises of the by-laws on file with them, and those operations must be *exclusively* not-for-profit. This doesn't mean that you can't publish, exhibit, perform, and so on—simply that any profits be applied to programs that support the stated purpose.

☐ The IRS wants to make sure that your programs are for *public* good, not *private* gain, and may look at indirect benefits that organizers of the association achieve through its good works.

☐ Political activity by the association is strictly forbidden. Again, this means by the organization as such, not that its founders and members have to check out of the political process. But mishaps like endorsing a candidate—or *appearing* to—can bring swift and terrible retribution.

☐ *Draft and adopt articles of association and by-laws.* You should check out boilerplate articles and by-laws from the library, buy one of the inexpensive handbooks available at bookstores with a business and technical section or, perhaps best of all, ask to look at the articles and by-laws of an existing association in your field. The articles of association—or organizational constitution—should give the association's name, state what it was set up to do, name the principal office, adopt Robert's Rules of Order as the parliamentary authority and describe procedures for election of directors and amendment of by-laws. In the case of the nonprofit association the directors and membership may be identical, and that's okay. Another good idea is a by-law that says no member will profit as an individual from money the organization secures and that, if and when you cease operations, some other nonprofit organization will be named to receive your assets, if any. The by-laws are a supplement to your articles or constitution, naming the roster of officers and their roles; establishing frequency, attendance and quorum rules for your meetings (law requires at least one a year), and settling bookkeeping details. A vital, final clause is one that says directors and members are exempt from liability as a result of the actions of the organization as a whole.

☐ *Apply for IRS tax exemption.* Warning: this approval may take up to *four months* to secure. In some cases you can apply for grants by describing your nonprofit status as "pending," but that's never a help, and may be a hindrance. The IRS publishes a brief guide called *How to Apply for and Retain Exempt Status for Your Organization,* IRS Publication 557, $1.20 from Superintendent of Documents, U.S. Government Printing Office, Washington, DC 20402. The form you'll use is IRS Form 1023, and with your first filing most of its spaces will be delightfully blank. But read them carefully, because they'll be answered in great detail in your annual reports to the government. You'll have to attach copies of your articles, by-laws, officers' roster and budget, if any, as well. Unless a third of your money comes from a single source, you'll probably be classed as a "public charity," which is the higher, more desirable category of deductibility. (The other sort of charity is the private foundation, the kind you may be asking for money, but the IRS is trying to crack down on rich people who use foundations to shelter assets and feed their hobbyhorses. If direct solicitation of gifts from individuals or from corporations who give without foundations is part of your over-all fundraising picture, you'll want to keep these distinctions in mind. Remember, too, that if you're a small nonprofit association—and the same applies to nonprofit corporations—a large gift from a single source can tilt you into the private foundation category, diminishing your tax attractiveness to certain givers.) You'll also have to fill out a form SS-4, Application for Employer Identification Number. Don't bother trying to tell the IRS you don't intend to have employees. You have to have the number anyway.

☐ *File appropriate state and local papers.* These requirements vary from state to state, but all states and territories have them. Generally, the paperwork involves notifying your Attorney General, Secretary of State, and in a handful of cases county or city authorities, that you exist. It's absolutely essential to do this and a lawyer or existing nonprofit association can help you find out what's necessary where you live.

Incorporation

The above checklist, describing nonprofit associations, covers most of the work involved in incorporation, and organizations that have met these standards can step up to corporate status simply by filing the additional paperwork.

Why incorporate?

- Corporations look a little more serious to proposal readers, and your hand may be strengthened.

- Corporations don't go out of existence for failing to meet annually and carry out their goals. They're imaginary "persons" in the eyes of the law, but persons who can be frozen and stored for revival and later use.

- Indemnification against liability of individual directors or participants for actions of the corporation generally is stronger than in the case of the *ad hoc* association.

- Corporate status will help qualify you for special low-cost mailing rates from the U.S. Postal Service, a cost-cutting must for many groups.

Checklist: steps to forming a nonprofit corporation

☐ *Qualification standards: IRS.* They're the same as described in the preceding checklist, and the same IRS publication provides a guide to the paperwork.

☐ *Articles of Incorporation and By-Laws.* Again, bookstore boilerplate or papers from an existing organization that closely matches the one you plan are the best guide. An intelligent tactic is to enlist the services of a cooperative lawyer as a member of your incorporation committee and/or board of directors.

☐ *State and local paperwork.* Corporations are natives of the states in which they're born, and if you go the corporation route you'll need your state and local approvals before securing IRS exemption. These procedures vary from state to state and will require local advice. As an idea of what lies ahead, the most populous state, California, requires the following steps:

  ☐ Reservation of corporate name through the California Secretary of State's Office.

  ☐ Tax-exemption claim to the California Franchise Tax Board. Tax board approval is required before you may . . .

  ☐ File articles of incorporation with the Secretary of State.

☐ File these same papers with the clerk of the California county in which the corporation conducts its affairs.

Remember that these steps are only an example and apply to *California*'s laws and regulations. You'll need to learn those in force where you live and you must meet them completely in order to secure the vital IRS exemption.

There are other special legal obligations faced by nonprofit corporations that have paid staff members, own property or sell things:

☐ Nonprofit corporations that employ people face the general obligations of all employers, including:

☐ Contributions to Social Security (FICA). This offers your staffers the retirement, disability, Medicare and survivor benefits everyone is familiar with. However, for corporations recognized by the IRS as tax-exempt, participation is elective, not mandatory. (But that means on a whole-organization, not employee-by-employee basis.) Corporations that do participate split the payments with their workers.

☐ Contributions to state welfare, unemployment and disability funds, which usually will be *mandatory*.

☐ Withholding of federal income taxes as part of payroll procedure. A special note here: some nonprofit organizations that are funded by a variety of sources face severe cash-flow problems, meaning that money is on the way, but doesn't arrive in time to cover urgent obligations. Since federal taxes withheld from payroll generally remain available until sent to the government, usually on a quarterly basis, these deposits sometimes become a tempting source of interest-free, short-term loans that require no collateral. Avoid this temptation. It can cost you your IRS exemption, and, at worst, lead to criminal prosecution. The best idea is to segregate the money into an escrowed account withheld for that purpose.

(One way to avoid these employer's obligations is to avoid "employees." You do this by treating the people who receive money from you as independent contractors, responsible for their own welfare and their own taxes. In the most recent past, the IRS has shown intense interest in controlling the use of this ploy. If they determine that your independent contractors aren't so independent, after all, but are actually working subject to an employer's direction, you'll have no choice. Already, monies paid such contractors are reported to the IRS, and the IRS was, at the end of 1980, pushing legislation to require withholding of independent contractors' taxes.)

☐ Nonprofit corporations that own property may or may not be considered exempt from state and local property taxes. Your incorporation papers and IRS exemption provide the basis for your local application for exemption, but it's essential to secure that exemption before actually purchasing taxable property or equipment. (New York City's leading noncommercial radio station poured more than a million dollars into converting an old church into a splendid new broadcast center. They presumed the property was tax-exempt, but the state said no and won. The station was threatened with fiscal ruin, forced to abandon the facility and sell it for taxes. It's happened elsewhere, too.)

☐ Selling things or charging admission or other fees can render a nonprofit corporation liable for collection and payment of sales taxes. In some cities, counties and states, vendor's licenses are necessary any time money changes hands, even a one-time charity affair. Your county assessor or local office of the state tax board is the place to ask about these requirements. Remember, also, that selling services or things once your project is underway may change your status in the eyes of the IRS and threaten your tax exemption.

Demonstrating reassurance in the proposal

Endorsements are best demonstrated through an appendix or attachment to the proposal, perhaps with one or two references in the body of the case statement. Simply provide a cover page for the section, titled "Endorsements" if you're following that form, and saying something like: "The pages that follow represent endorsements of the project in this proposal by members and leaders of the community we intend to serve."

Formal shelter—the case in which an organization is administering the money you're asking for—requires only a one-page letter from a responsible officer of the institution describing what amounts to a simple business arrangement and, if the signer's name will carry weight, expressing hope that the proposal will be funded and stating how appropriate it is to that organization's general purposes.

Nonprofit association should be demonstrated by a copy of the IRS exemption letter, any similar letter from your state's taxing authority and, in the case of certain grants, submission of your articles of association, your by-laws and a list of your officers and directors.

Nonprofit corporations follow the same procedure as nonprofit associations. The state and local documents that deal with employee, sales and property tax matters are of little use in certain projects but if, for example, your proposal is for a grant for capital funds to build a plant for your project, demonstrating property tax exemption would be essential. The *key* document is the IRS letter of tax exemption. Your state certificate of incorporation may satisfy some givers that you've met the law; others will wish to see your articles, by-laws and roster of officers.

After the Proposal Is Written: Submission, Solicitation, Negotiation, Reporting, Follow-up

The written grant proposal is only a *part* of the total grant process. Far more important are the human factors involved in the project design, the first contacts with potential funding sources and finally the meetings and conversations that make you real in the prospect's eyes. These "people factors" remain important *after* you get the money, and winning the grant may, by law or custom, oblige you to do further writing and reporting tasks.

Deadlines and submission

One of the main jobs of prospect research is finding out as much as you can about the target prospect's deadlines—not merely the public one, the last day you can submit a proposal, but the private ones, the internal schedule for weighing the applications and deciding who gets the funding.

Most small foundations have no staff to help with this job. Instead, it's carried out by heirs to the estate that created the foundation, trust officers of a bank, members of a legal firm, or the officers of an organization that stands in for a formal board. In cases like this, the decisions often happen at one meeting a year, which in turn may be scheduled to match another meeting—such as that of the founding company's board of directors. In other cases, the decisions happen in December, just before the close of the tax year.

In government grants, the process is always formal and begins with a staff-level reading of the proposal to determine whether all the legal hurdles have been cleared, merits of the project aside. After that, the government agency may send the proposal to program specialists on its own staff or to outside bodies, such as review boards of experts within your field or staff members of state or local authorities (including those who already may have ranked your proposal against their state plan). Finally comes the series of internal funding conferences in which competing applications are weighed and the decisions handed down.

In either case—private or public money—your prospect research should have revealed to you the name of the insider who has the job of shepherding your proposal through the maze. Make this person an ally and, without turning into a bloody nuisance, call at intervals for reports on precisely where your paperwork currently is within the administrative stream.

If you've conferred with the insider *before* filing, you already may have modified your draft proposal on the basis of his or her advice. Your finished proposal should go in as early as possible, well in advance of the deadline. If you've met the legal standards and your work circulates among staff at this early stage of the game, it becomes the proposal against which later submissions are measured. (No funding group I've ever heard of issues points for promptness, and the great bulk of proposals will arrive at the last qualifying moment, but the practical merit of getting in early is plain.)

How about getting in late? Perhaps a local corporate or private foundation with which you've developed extraordinary rapport would permit this; government agencies, by rule, do not. Some allow informal grace periods of twelve hours, by postmark, but the best way to get your foot in the door at the last minute is to use metered postage issued before the fatal midnight. Most parcel postage sold at the post office comes from meters, and meter-stripped mail bears its own date.

Solicitation

The techniques of general fundraising include a procedure for submitting your proposal in person—solicitation—and it can be an especially effective way of dealing with small and staff-less private foundations and corporate givers.

This is also the best use of the people you have listed as outside contacts. It's almost a ritual, and treat it as one, because breaking the "rule of two" can be fatal.

Checklist: filing your proposal in person

☐ The "rule of two" decrees that the job be done by two persons—no more, no less. One of the persons is close to the funding authority, such as one of your board members who has friends or a seat on the target's board. The other is someone well acquainted with the project, such as you, who wrote the proposal.

☐ Write or phone for a personal appointment at the target's usual place of business, during regular business hours. Avoid invitations to meet for breakfast, lunch, on the 16th tee—anywhere except a place where your target is fully-focused on the matters you want to discuss.

☐ At the meeting, explain your proposal and the steps you've taken to assure that it matches the target's giving goals. If the target appears willing to scan the proposal with you, do so. If not, leave it and leave—quickly, saying that you'll soon be back in touch for their decision, or, if their deadline is clear to you, will await their decision with hope.

☐ In cases where the decision is made on a proposal-by-proposal basis—often the case with small foundations and corporations—have the senior member of the soliciting team call two or three days later for a second meeting under the same circumstances as the first. If the target or an aide offers the information that you've lost out, make it clear that you want to be told so in person. (The implication is that you'll be insulted if you are not.) If the answer is a firm *no*, follow up with a thank-you note asking for specific information about why you lost and whether it would be useless to apply later. If the firm *no* is delivered in person, do the same—in person. If the answer is *maybe*, you're negotiating, and there's a section later in this chapter about how to deal with that. If the answer is *yes, but* we're giving you less than you asked for—*try* to get into negotiations for the higher figure. If the answer is a firm *yes, but*—make clear your disappointment with the lower figure and the problems it poses, and then immediately offer the gratitude that's truly due.

Negotiation

Not often, but sometimes, a funding source will tell you that you *almost* have the money. Except.

"Except" can be a lot of different things. Perhaps they've decided to approach a group of applicants and ask each to pare the budget so all can share what's available. Perhaps they want you to change some aspect of your proposal, such as the staffing level.

When the changes proposed are technical and reasonable, you should be willing to enter negotiations in good faith. (Never mind whether the conversations are called that; they are.) If they're asking you to tinker with your philosophy or to make big changes in your attack on the problem you want to solve, that's another matter. In the case of large projects, negotiation can make your role as fundraiser uncomfortable. Your colleagues may view you as an advocate of compromise, and some degree of compromise may indeed be necessary.

But it is generally considered a poor idea to recast your project to match a funding source's needs. Faulty prospect research is one matter, but a money target who changes the rules during the game is another. Search for logic in the changes proposed, but if it appears to you that this is a matter of a power play, of what used to be called co-optation, you may wish to bow out gracefully and look for funds elsewhere.

Three thoughts about negotiating on proposals, should it happen to you:

- Negotiations mean you're close, and should mean that both sides are willing to give a little.

- How much give you're willing to offer has to be decided by yourself, or in counsel with colleagues, ahead of the negotiating meetings.

- And the negotiations *should* happen in a meeting, or meetings, that open with a quick summary of the problem areas and move immediately to a step-by-step discussion of each. In such meetings, it's wise to follow the "rule of two" and rely on the presence of one of your outside connections, somebody who's well-known to the other side, to help you. Never negotiate when outnumbered. If their committee has five members, so should your delegation.

Reporting

All grants carry an obligation to report what happened to the money and the project, whether it is stated in writing or law or not at all.

In the case of individual grants, the report may be a copy of the finished project in printed form, slides of artwork, tape or videotape of performance, and so on. In fact, the requirement for documentation in arts grants has helped to create a whole class of art-worker whose technique consists of documenting things, an interesting and often amusing merging of funding process and finished product. On larger projects, standards for internal and external review should be agreed upon as part of project design and written into your proposals.

The most formal and daunting sort of program review is the on-site inspection by officials of government funding bodies. These rarely occur un-announced, but most government applications mention them somewhere in the fine print, and you should conduct your project as though one could happen at any time. When they *do* happen, you'll find that the inspecting officials are realists who acknowledge the practical differences between plans on paper and projects in operation. But they're also a little like the parents of your project; they want to be proud of it and will become defensive, or worse, if you're less than forthcoming with them. Inspections don't give the visiting officials the right to scour your working files, interview staff members or facility-users without your presence, or in general assert ownership of something they've merely contributed to. In some cases the inspecting officials may be visiting because they know, or suspect, that your project is among the handful whose books or facilities will be the target of a general audit by higher government authorities—such as accountants at the Secretary level of their department, who are trying to assess the overall honesty and efficiency of a whole funding program. The author has been involved in inspections in which the on-site visit ratified the needs stated in our proposals, proved our ability to make the most of limited resources and resulted in a commitment to higher levels of support in the years ahead. If it happens to you, view it as the greatest selling opportunity of all—a walk-through of your project itself with people who can do you a world of good in the future.

Assessing the success of your program usually is a value judgment, but remember that you're dealing with money managers, and the financial records are something else again. Almost without exception, government grants reserve the right to conduct audits at any time, and with projects of a certain, large, size, they should be considered inevitable. Smaller government grants, foundation and corporate grants usually are made with the expectation of one or more financial reports, generally in the middle of the funded period and at the end. But the only way to maintain fiscal sanity is to keep the books as you go along. Reconstructing them against a reporting deadline or in the presence of angry auditors is grief nobody needs.

Crash course: bookkeeping
and accounting for grant recipients

Bookkeeping and accounting are two different things, and while almost any-one capable of writing a grant proposal can organize bookkeeping records, accounting,—the preparation of statements of assets and liabilities that exactly balance—requires somebody trained in accounting. As an individual or small organization, you should seek the volunteer services of an accountant who could serve on your board, perhaps as treasurer, or work alongside your project. In the case of grants sheltered by a larger institution, you may be asked to help a member of the financial staff review records of the money side of your work on a periodic basis.

What records do you need?

A cash receipts journal, that gives the date received, amount and source of the money you get.

A cash disbursements journal, that shows every instance of money *leaving* the project. Items such as payroll and petty cash deserve, for different reasons, separate, fine records of their own, but should be shown leaving your cash disbursements journal either in block payments, or on a check-by-check basis. Even if your organization winds up with several bank accounts, this is the master source for recording cash on its way out of your hands.

A general journal, that records transactions that don't involve cash, such as the receipt of gifts-in-kind (accounting services, for example), of real property, and so on. Services and properties should be entered according to their fair market value, and your receipt to the donor should exactly match your journal entry value. Why? Because the donor will be claiming a tax deduction. The emphasis in "fair market value" should be on "fair." Inflating the worth of such gifts is a violation of tax statutes.

A general ledger that summarizes records from the three journals above and gives you a handy survey of your financial picture.

Checkbook records, cancelled checks, and *receipts* that match the journal entries and are essential in an audit. It's also a good idea to make photocopies of the grant checks you receive.

All of the above records will give your accountant the data he or she needs to prepare financial statements. These records are vital to cash basis accounting, the simpler form. For the more complex and accurate accrual basis accounting, your accountant will need records of accounts receivable (who owes you what and when) and accounts payable (whom you owe what and when). Considered on a regular basis, such as monthly or quarterly, these additional accounts will give you the total money picture and satisfy any auditor. Using these data, the accountant can prepare statements of assets and liabilities that reveal your positive or negative net worth, and statements of revenues and expenses in which your operating profit or loss is revealed. Profits aren't illegal in nonprofit organizations; they simply have to be applied to your tax-exempt purposes, and mean essentially only that you spent less, or got more, than expected. A rare occurrence.

Another good accounting tool is a statement that sets forth in short form your sources and use of revenues, including all of the income to the project and loans carried in its name. This gives potential grantors proof of your success in spreading the cost of your operations appropriately among diverse sources.

And a final, vital accounting from the management perspective is the *cash-flow statement,* which splits your budget into segments—monthly is usual—and compares obligations with the cash actually available to cover them. For example, if your payroll, rent, debt retirement and so on amount to $12,000 a month, and a $60,000 federal grant appears on your income side, you can still go out of business if the grant isn't paid in time. Lines on both sides of this statement should be brutally summarized. When people talk about the bottom-line in nonprofit management, the bottom line that counts is the cash-flow in the current month, and the money managers will expect you to have prepared a cash-flow statement in all but the tiniest projects.

Sometimes nonprofit organizations seek loans to get themselves through cash droughts, but aside from the largesse of wealthy individuals, you're going to need collateral, the organization's real property. Real property appears on your project inventory, which your accountant will depreciate each year to reflect the declining resale value of the stuff as it gets old. Many government grants forbid you to use equipment purchased with taxpayer money as collateral for loans to provide operating funds.

If you haven't learned what kind of financial records a funding source expects you to keep, make it a point to ask the moment you hear the good news. In government grants, the news about reporting standards generally is contained up-front, in your original application and its instructions.

Nonprofit associations and corporations—any group with IRS tax exemption—are obliged to summarize their financial picture each year on the form 990-AR, the same one described as a tool for you in looking for money back in the prospect research section.

Briefly summarized, the IRS demands that you:

- Reveal receipts, expenses and disbursements, resulting in assets, liabilities and net worth positions for the beginning and the end of the calendar year.

- Declare that you haven't changed your activities without revealing so to the IRS, that you haven't engaged in lobbying, that you have obeyed federal requirements about nondiscrimination and haven't suffered "liquidation, dissolution, termination, or substantial contraction," which you must explain if you have.

- (In cases where organizations handled gross receipts of over $25,000 a year) summarize income sources, expenses and disbursements in a way reminiscent of personal tax returns, and provide balance sheets showing your situation at the beginning and the end of the tax year.

Follow-up

Reporting on your project is more than merely polite. It makes good sense for your future. Accounting records are important to the money managers, but so is a more subjective sense of what's going on, and a narrative account—an updated case statement—is the best way to provide it. If you work with a board of directors that meets regularly, project reviews prepared for the minutes can provide the groundwork for this document. A regular newsletter for supporters is a good idea. It reminds them of your existence and their contribution, again and again. Send it to: all the names on your insiders and outside connections lines on the prospect research form, all of your board members, those who provided written endorsements and advice for the proposal, and all those you'd like to see playing one of these roles. Once a foundation or corporation has given you money, you should have no qualms about breaking with protocol and adding additional board members or executives to your mailing list. If you've intelligently cultivated mentors, colleagues and funders with staff support, those staff members who have helped you should be kept up-to-date, too.

Individual grant recipients should follow these procedures in a simpler fashion: letters to backers with reports of work in progress, copies of published findings, or reviews of performances, publications or exhibits. In general, share your successes, showing how the picture you painted with your proposal is coming true, thanks to them.

Some grant and fundraising counselors advise remembering the birthdays and anniversaries of funding executives, or sending them holiday cards. This seems to me a bit mechanical and may be met with the response calculated cheer usually engenders—the synthetic warmth of the drugstore advertising calendar. Friends you've made playing the grants game should be treated like friends.

Maintenance and recycling

As you've seen, the grants game is a 24-hour-a-day, year-long endeavor. Unless your needs are surprisingly fleeting or your initial success historically immense, you'll have to stay in shape to stay in competition.

By the end of the game, your four simple file folders should have multiplied into a living system:

- *Prospect research files,* divided between the sources you applied to and the new leads you're developing. Keep filling out prospect research forms and, well before the funding body's own giving cycle begins again, arrange for a call or meeting to learn whether it makes sense for you to apply again, whether their goals have changed, what you can do to win this time around.

- *The case statement and its supporting evidence.* Files for drafts of the case statement for the proposals you'll write in your next fiscal year or, for projects too small for a fiscal year, the next time you ask for a grant. You should keep duplicate pages of the latest statement, budget and so on, for use in unexpected grant opportunities and to explain yourself to potential members of your support network.

- *The reassurance files* should be upgraded constantly by new letters, or pledges of letters, from new endorsers, copies of your latest reports to the various government bodies overseeing your nonprofit status and the financial records that ratify the match between your earlier plans and your actual operations.

- *Your follow-through files* should record the full extent of the support network you've developed inside and outside the funding bodies and the reports you're making to them on a constant basis. Of all the files, they're the most important, the ones that acknowledge the rule all grants game winners know in their hearts: people give money to people.

Part Three:
APPENDIXES

Appendix One:
Prospect Research Resources

Here, drawn from Foundation Center listings and updated early in 1981 by the staff of *The Grants Game,* is a state-by-state directory of foundation research centers and handbooks.

Keep in mind that local directories often reflect out-of-date information about funding patterns, and in some cases will list departed staff and board members. You should write or phone the publisher before ordering to see whether the book is still in print and how much it costs now.

Many of the research centers and special collections listed below conduct seminars and workshops for newcomers to the grants game. (All four operated directly by The Foundation Center do so.) These special centers are the best single source of information about the increasingly important smaller local foundations and should be considered well worth an out-of-town trip for consultation.

ALABAMA

Birmingham Public Library
2020 Park Place
Birmingham, AL 35203   (205) 254-2541

Auburn University at Montgomery Library
Montgomery, AL 36117   (205) 279-9110

A Guide to Foundations of the Southeast, Vol. IV, Jerry C. Davis, editor.
Davis-Taylor Associates. 1976. (Out of print; consult library copy.)

ALASKA

University of Alaska, Anchorage
Library
3211 Providence Drive
Anchorage, AL 99504   (907) 263-1848

ARIZONA

Phoenix Public Library
Social Sciences Subject Dept.
12 East McDowell Road.
Phoenix, AZ 85004   (602) 262-4782

Tucson Public Library
200 South Sixth Avenue
Tucson, AZ 85701   (602) 791-4393

ARKANSAS

Westark Community College Library
Grand Avenue at Waldron Road
Fort Smith, AR 72913   (501) 785-4241

Little Rock Public Library
Reference Department
700 Louisiana Street
Little Rock, AR 72201   (501) 374-7546

A Guide to Foundations of the Southeast, Vol. IV, Jerry C. Davis, editor. Davis-Taylor Associates. 1976. (Out of print; consult library copy.)

CALIFORNIA

The Foundation Center
312 Sutter Street
San Francisco, CA 94108   (415) 397-0902

Edward L. Doheny Memorial Library
University of Southern California
Los Angeles, CA 90007   (213) 741-2540

San Diego Public Library
820 E Street
San Diego, CA 92101   (714) 236-5816

San Francisco Business Library
(San Francisco Public Library branch)
530 Kearny Street
San Francisco, CA 94108   (415) 558-3946

Santa Barbara Public Library Reference Section
40 East Anapamu, P.O. Box 1019
Santa Barbara, CA 93102   (805) 962-7653

Guide to California Foundations. San Francisco Study Center. 1978. 294 pages. $6 from Guide to California Foundations, P.O. Box 5646, San Francisco, CA 94101. Make check payable to Northern California Foundations Group.

Small Change from Big Bucks: A Report and Recommendations on Bay Area Foundations and Social Change. Herb Allen and Sam Sternberg, editors. Bay Area Committee for Responsive Philanthropy. 1979. 226 pages. $6 from the Committee at 944 Market Street, San Francisco, CA 94102. Make check payable to Regional Young Adult Project.

Where the Money's At, How to Reach Over 500 California Grant-Making Foundations. Patricia Blair Tobey, editor, with Irving R. Warner. ICPR Publications. 1978. 536 pages. $17 from ICPR Publications, 9255 Sunset Boulevard, 8th Floor, Los Angeles, CA 90069.

COLORADO

Denver Public Library
Sociology Division
1357 Broadway
Denver, CO 80203   (303) 573-5152

Colorado Foundation Directory. 2nd Edition. Junior League of Denver, Denver Foundation, Attorney General of Colorado. 1980. 61 pages. Based on state and federal returns and information volunteered by approximately 192 foundations. Appendixes list foundations by assets, grants and fields of interest. $7 from Junior League of Denver, Inc., 1805 South Bellaire, Suite 400, Denver, CO 80222. Make check payable to Colorado Foundation Directory.

CONNECTICUT

Hartford Public Library
Reference Department
500 Main Street
Hartford, CT 06103   (203) 525-9121

A Directory of Foundations in the State of Connecticut. John Parker Huber, editor. 1976. 168 pages. Based on 1973 IRS forms 990 from 590 Foundations, arranged alphabetically. Indexes by area, purpose and largest single grants. $8 billed, $7 prepaid, from Eastern Connecticut State College Foundation, Inc., P.O. Box 431, Willimantic, CT 06226.

1979 Connecticut Foundation Directory. Michael E. Burns, editor. 1979. 92 pages. Based on 1977 and 1978 IRS forms 990, arranged alphabetically by 465 foundations, no indexes. $10 prepaid from DATA, 1 State Street, New Haven, CT 06511.

DELAWARE

Hugh Morris Library
University of Delaware
Newark, DE 19711   (302) 738-2965

Delaware Foundations. United Way of Delaware, Inc., compiler. 1979. 116 pages. Based on 1976–78 IRS forms 990, annual reports and information from 558 foundations, arranged alphabetically. Includes 96 private foundations, some company-sponsored foundations and corporate programs, 24 operating foundations and 438 out-of-state foundations. No indexes. $7.50 prepaid from United Way of Delaware, Inc., 701 Shipley Street, Wilmington, DE 19801.

DISTRICT OF COLUMBIA

The Foundation Center
11001 Connecticut Avenue, N.W.
Washington, DC 20036   (202) 331-1400

The Washington, D.C., Metropolitan Area Foundation Directory. Julia Mills Jacobsen and Kay Carter Courtade, editors. 1979. 80 pages. Based on 1976–77 IRS forms 990 and information from the foundations. Separate sections list non-grantmaking foundations, operating foundations, inactive foundations and dissolved foundations. Indexes of foundation names and of officers and trustees. $13.50 from Management Communications, Publications Division, 4416 Edmunds Street, N.W., Washington, DC 20007.

The Guide to Washington, D.C. Foundations. 2nd Edition. Francis de Bettencourt, editor. 1975. 58 pages. Alphabetical listing of 282 foundations, based on 1973 IRS forms 990. Index of officers. $8 from Guide Publishers, P.O. Box 5849, Washington, DC 20014.

FLORIDA

Jacksonville Public Library
Business, Science and Industry Department
122 North Ocean Street
Jacksonville, FL 32202   (904) 633-3926

Miami-Dade Public Library
Florida Collection
One Biscayne Boulevard
Miami, FL 33132   (305) 579-5001

A Guide to Foundations of the Southeast, Vol. III. Jerry C. Davis, editor. 1975. 309 pages. Alphabetical listing of 487 foundations, officer index. Published by Davis-Taylor Associates. (Out of print; consult library copy.)

GEORGIA

Atlanta Public Library
1 Margaret Mitchell Square at Forsyth and Carnegie Way
Atlanta, GA 30303   (404) 688-4636

Georgia Foundation Directory. Ann Bush, compiler. 1979. 28 pages. Alphabetical listing of approximately 550 foundations, geographic listing by foundation name and subject listing by foundation name. No indexes, addresses not included. Free from Foundation Collection, Atlanta Public Library, 10 Pryor Street, S.W., Atlanta, GA 30303.

Guide to Foundations in Georgia. Georgia Department of Human Resources, compiler. 1978. 145 pages. Alphabetical listing of 530 foundations based on 1975–77 IRS forms 990. Indexes of foundation names, cities, program interests. Free from State Economic Opportunity Unit, Office of District Programs, Department of Human Resources, 618 Ponce de Leon Avenue, N.E., Atlanta, GA 30308.

A Guide to Foundations of the Southeast, Vol. III. Jerry C. Davis, editor. 1975. 309 pages. Alphabetical listing of 340 Georgia foundations, officer index. Published by Davis-Taylor Associates. (Out of print; consult library copy.)

HAWAII

Thomas Hale Hamilton Library
University of Hawaii
Humanities and Social Sciences Division
2550 The Mall
Honolulu, HI 96822   (808) 948-7214

IDAHO

Caldwell Public Library
1010 Dearborn Street
Caldwell, ID 83605   (208) 459-3242

Directory of Idaho Foundations. Caldwell Public Library. 1978. 8 pages. Alphabetical listing of 49 foundations, based mostly upon 1977–78 IRS forms 990. Includes assets, grants and major areas of interest. No indexes. $1 prepaid from The Foundation Collection, Caldwell Public Library, 1010 Dearborn Street, Caldwell, ID 83605.

ILLINOIS

Donors Forum of Chicago
208 South LaSalle Street
Chicago, IL 60604   (312) 726-4882

Sangamon State University Library
Shepherd Road
Springfield, IL 62708   (217) 786-6633

Illinois Foundation Directory Beatrice J. Capriotti and Frank J. Capriotti III, editors. 1978. 527 pages. Based on 1976–77 IRS forms 990, plus correspondence with foundations. Main section lists approximately 1900 foundations alphabetically. No indexes. $425 from Foundation Data Center, 100 Wesley Temple Building, 123 East Grant Street, Minneapolis, MN 55403.

INDIANA

Indianapolis-Marion County Public Library
40 East St. Clair Street
Indianapolis, IN 46204   (311) 635-5662

Indiana Foundations: A Directory Paula Reading Spear, editor. 1979. 175 pages. Alphabetical listing of 265 foundations, based on 1977–79 IRS forms 990. Indexes of financial criteria, subject and county, restricted foundations, foundations for student assistance only and dissolved foundations. $19.95 prepaid from Central Research Systems, 320 North Meridian, Suite 1011, Indianapolis, IN 46204.

IOWA

Public Library of Des Moines
100 Locust Street
Des Moines, IA, 50309   (515) 283-4259

KANSAS

Topeka Public Library
Adult Services Department
1515 West Tenth Street
Topeka, KS 66604   (913) 233-2040

Directory of Kansas Foundations. Connie Townsley, editor. 1979. 128 pages. Alphabetical listing of approximately 255 foundations, based on IRS forms 990. (Date of information not given.) City index. $5.80 prepaid from Association of Community Arts Councils of Kansas, Columbian Building, 4th Floor, 112 West Sixth Street, Topeka, KS 66603.

Directory of Kansas Foundations, 2nd Edition. Molly Wisman, editor. 1977. Unpaged. Predecessor (despite edition number) to the guide listed above, and based on 1976 IRS forms 990. $1.25 from Association of Community Arts Councils of Kansas, Columbian Building, 4th Floor, 112 West Sixth Street, Topeka, KS 66603.

KENTUCKY

Louisville Free Public Library
Fourth and York Streets
Louisville, KY 40203   (502) 584-4154

A Guide to Foundations of the Southeast, Volume I. Jerry C. Davis, editor. 1975. 255 pages. Alphabetical listing of 119 foundations, based on 1976 IRS forms 990. Index of officers. Published by Davis-Taylor Associates. (Out of print; consult library copy.)

LOUISIANA

East Baton Rouge Parish Library
Centroplex Library
120 East St. Louis Street
Baton Rouge, LA 70802   (504) 344-5291

New Orleans Public Library
Business and Science Division
219 Loyola Avenue
New Orleans, LA 70140   (504) 586-4919

A Guide to Foundations of the Southeast, Vol. IV. Jerry C. Davis, editor. 1976. 165 pages. Alphabetical listing of 172 foundations, based on 1973–74 IRS forms 990. Index of officers. Published by Davis-Taylor Associates. (Out of print; consult library copy.)

MAINE

University of Southern Maine
Center for Research and Advanced Study
246 Deering Avenue
Portland, ME 04102   (207) 780-4411

A Directory of Foundations in the State of Maine, 2nd edition. Center for Research and Advanced Study. 1979. 59 pages. Alphabetical listing of 161 foundations, based on 1978 IRS forms 990. Sections on grant writing, bibliography, description of IRS information returns, foundation listings by city or town. No indexes. $3 prepaid from Center for Research and Advanced Study, University of Southern Maine, 246 Deering Avenue, Portland, ME 04102.

MARYLAND

Enoch Pratt Free Library
Social Science and History Department
400 Cathedral Street
Baltimore, MD 21201   (301) 396-5320

1977 Annual Index Foundation Reports. Office of the Attorney General. 1978. 39 pages. Alphabetical listing of approximately 300 foundations, based on 1977 IRS forms 990 received by the Maryland Attorney General. $5 prepaid from Office of the Attorney General, One South Calvert Street, 12th Floor, Baltimore, MD 21202. Attention: Sharon Smith.

MASSACHUSETTS

Associated Foundation of Greater Boston
294 Washington Street, Suite 501
Boston, MA 02108   (617) 426-2608

Boston Public Library
Copley Square
Boston, MA 02117   (617) 536-5400

Community Grants Resource Catalogue: A Directory of Philanthropic Foundations in the Commonwealth of Massachusetts. Steve Rubin, Don Levitan, editors. 1977. 82 pages. Alphabetical listing of 433 foundations, based on 1973 IRS forms 990. Index of subjects. $9 from Government Research Publications, Box 122, Newton Center, MA 02159.

Directory Of Foundations in Massachusetts. Office of the Attorney General of the Commonwealth of Massachusetts and Associated Foundations of Greater Boston. 1977. 135 pages. Lists 726 foundations, based on 1975 IRS forms 990 and separated between foundations that make grants primarily to organizations and those that make grants primarily to individuals. Appendixes of grant amounts, geographic restrictions, purposes, loans, nonscholarship loans, scholarships restricted by city, scholarships; population groups and scholarships; purpose restricted. $7.50 prepaid from University of Massachusetts Press, Box 429, Amherst, MA 01002.

A Directory of Foundations in the Commonwealth of Massachusetts. John Parker Huber, editor. 2nd edition, 1976. 161 pages. Main section lists 960 foundations alphabetically, based on 1974 IRS forms 990. Indexes by geographical areas and largest grants awarded. $15 prepaid from Eastern Connecticut State College Foundation, Inc., P.O. Box 431, Willimantic, CT 06226.

Directory of the Major Greater Boston Area Foundations. 1974. 42 pages. Alphabetical listing of 47 foundations in the Boston area, based on 1972 IRS forms 990. $14.95, plus postage, from J. F. Gray Company, P.O. Box 748, Islington Station, Westwood, MA 02090.

MICHIGAN

Alpena County Library
211 North First Avenue
Alpena, MI 49707   (517) 356-6188

Henry Ford Centennial Library
16301 Michigan Avenue
Dearborn, MI 48126   (313) 943-2337

Purdy Library
Wayne State University
Detroit, MI 48202   (313) 577-4040

Michigan State University Libraries
Reference Library
East Lansing, MI 48824   (517) 353-8826

University of Michigan—Flint: UM—F Library
Reference Department
Flint, MI 48503   (313) 762-3408

Grand Rapids Public Library
Sociology and Education Dept.
Library Plaza
Grand Rapids, MI 49502   (616) 456-4411

Michigan Technological University Library
Highway U.S. 41
Houghton, MI 49931   (906) 487-2507

Directory of Foundations in the State of Michigan. Janet C. Huber, editor. 1974. 123 pages. Alphabetical listing of 696 foundations, based on 1972 IRS forms 990. Indexes of foundations by cities and purpose of grants. $10 from Dunham Pond Press, Storrs, CT 06268.

The Michigan Foundation Directory, 3rd edition. Council of Michigan Foundations and Michigan League for Human Services. 1980. 113 pages.

Based on 1978 IRS forms 990 and information from The Foundation Center, lists 863 foundations, 304 of which have assets of $200,000 or make annual grants of at least $25,000; brief data on 774 foundations that make grants of $1,000 or more annually; geographical listing of foundations by city, of terminated foundations and of special-purpose foundations. Includes a survey of Michigan giving patterns and information for grant-seekers. Indexes by subject, donor, trustee, officer, foundation name. $9 prepaid from Michigan League for Human Services, 200 Mill Street, Lansing, MI 48933.

MINNESOTA

Minneapolis Public Library
Sociology Department
300 Nicollet Mall
Minneapolis, MN 55401   (612) 372-6555

Guide to Minnesota Foundations. Minnesota Council on Foundations. 1977. 73 pages. Alphabetical listing of 571 grant-making foundations, operating foundations, scholarship and educational foundations, recently dissolved foundations, largest foundations. Based on 1975 IRS forms 990. Appendix listing grants by out-of-state foundations to Minnesota organizations. $10 from Minnesota Council on Foundations, Foshay Tower, Suite 413, Ninth and Marquette Avenues, Minneapolis, MN 55402.

Minnesota Foundation Directory. Beatrice J. Capriotti and Frank J. Capriotti III, editors. 1976. 274 pages. Alphabetical listing of 598 foundations, based on 1973–74 IRS forms 990. Indexes of donors, administrators and trustees, banks and trust companies as corporate trustees. $250 from Minnesota Foundation Directory, 101 Boy Scouts of America Building, 5300 Glenwood Avenue North, Minneapolis, MN 55442.

Minnesota Foundation Directory III: Guidelines and Deadlines. Beatrice J. Capriotti, editor. 1976. 105 pages. Lists 55 foundations alphabetically; based on 1973–75 IRS forms 990 and information from the foundations. $50 from Minnesota Foundation Directory III, Peavey Building, Suite 305, Minneapolis, MN 55402.

MISSISSIPPI

Jackson Metropolitan Library
301 North State Street
Jackson, MI 39201   (601) 994-1120

A Guide to Foundations of the Southeast: Volume IV. Jerry C. Davis, editor
1976. 165 pages. Lists 68 foundations, based on 1973–75 IRS forms 990. Pub
lished by Davis-Taylor Associates, Inc. (Out of print; consult library copy.)

MISSOURI

Clearinghouse for Mid-Continent Foundations
University of Missouri, Kansas City Law School
Suite 1-300
52nd Street and Oak
Kansas City, MO 64113   (816) 276-1176

Kansas City Public Library
311 East 12th Street
Kansas City, MO 64106   (816) 221-2685

Metropolitan Association for Philanthropy, Inc.
5600 Oakland, G-324
St. Louis, MO 63110   (314) 647-2290

Springfield-Greene County Library
397 East Central Street
Springfield, MO 65801   (417) 869-4621

MONTANA

Eastern Montana College Library
Reference Department
Billings, MT 59101   (406) 657-2320

NEBRASKA

W. Dale Clark Library
Social Sciences Department
215 South 15th Street
Omaha, NE 68102   (402) 444-4822

Nebraska Foundation Directory. Junior League of Omaha. 1979. 77 pages. Approximately 154 foundations, listed alphabetically and based on 1976–77 IRS forms 990. Free (limited supply) from Junior League of Omaha, 7365 Pacific Street, Omaha, NE 68114.

NEVADA

Clark County Library
1401 East Flamingo Road
Las Vegas, NV 89109   (702) 733-7810

Washoe County Library
301 South Center Street
Reno, NV 89505   (702) 785-4190

NEW HAMPSHIRE

The New Hampshire Charitable Fund
One South Street
P.O. Box 1335
Concord, NH 03301   (603) 225-6641

Directory of Charitable Funds in New Hampshire. Alphabetical listing of approximately 400 foundations, based on 1974–75 records filed with the state Attorney General. Indexes of geographical areas for foundations with restricted grants and of purposes when not geographically restricted. $2 (annual supplement, $1) from Office of the Attorney General, State House Annex, Concord, NH 03301.

NEW JERSEY

New Jersey State Library
Governmental Reference
185 West State Street
P.O.Box 1898
Trenton, NJ 08625   (609) 292-6220

Foundations in New Jersey: A Directory, 2nd edition. Governmental Reference office, Bureau of Law, Legislative and General Reference Services Division of the New Jersey State Library, Archives and History. 1978. Irregular paging. Lists 783 foundations, based on 1976–77 IRS forms 990. Two sections: alphabetical listing by foundation name with IRS number and county, and county listing by foundation name with address. Free (limited supply) from Governmental Reference Office, New Jersey State Library, P.O. Box 1898, Trenton, NJ 08625.

The New Jersey Mitchell Guide: Foundations, Corporations and Their Managers, 2nd edition. (A revised edition of *A Directory of New Jersey Foundations,* 1977). Janet A. Mitchell, editor. 1980. 218 pages. Alphabetical listing of 321 foundations and 374 corporations, based on 1977–78 IRS forms 990 and information supplied by the foundations, plus sections on corporations and scholarship foundations. Indexes of foundations and corporations by county and by managers. Appendixes list foundation statistics, foundations with grant totals over $100,000. $20 prepaid from The Mitchell Guides, P.O. Box 413, Princeton, NJ 08540.

NEW MEXICO

New Mexico State Library
300 Don Gaspar Street
Santa Fe, NM 87501   (505) 827-2033

NEW YORK

The Foundation Center
888 Seventh Avenue
New York, NY 10106   (212) 975-1120

New York State Library
Cultural Education Center
Humanities Section
Empire State Plaza
Albany, NY 12230   (518) 474-7645

Buffalo and Erie County Public Library
Lafayette Square
Buffalo, NY 14203   (716) 856-7525

Levittown Public Library
Reference Department
One Bluegrass Lane
Levittown, NY 11756   (516) 731-5728

Plattsburgh Public Library
Reference Department
15 Oak Street
Plattsburgh, NY 12901   (518) 563-0921

Rochester Public Library
Business and Social Division
115 South Avenue
Rochester, NY 14604   (716) 428-7328

Onondaga County Public Library
335 Montgomery Street
Syracuse, NY 13202   (315) 473-4491

New York Foundation Profiles. James H. Taylor, editor. 1976. 259 pages. Alphabetical listing of 950 foundations, based on 1974–75 IRS forms 990. $29.95 from Davis-Taylor Associates, Inc., Route 3, Box 289, Mt. Morgan Road, Williamsburg, KY 40769.

NORTH CAROLINA

North Carolina State Library
109 East Jones Street
Raleigh, NC 27611   (919) 733-3270

The Winston-Salem Foundation
229 First Union National Bank Building
Winston-Salem, NC 27101   (919) 725-2382

A Guide to Foundations of the Southeast: Volume II. Jerry C. Davis, editor.
Lists 415 North Carolina foundations, based on 1973–74 IRS forms 990. Published by Davis-Taylor Associates, Inc. (Out of print; consult library copy.)

NORTH DAKOTA

The Library
North Dakota State University
Fargo, ND 58105   (701) 237-8876

OHIO

The Foundation Center
Kent H. Smith Library
739 National City Bank Building
629 Euclid
Cleveland, OH 44114   (216) 861-1933

Public Library of Cincinnati and Hamilton County
Education Department
800 Vine Street
Cincinnati, OH 45202   (513) 369-6940

Toledo-Lucas County Public Library
Social Science Department

325 North Michigan Street
Toledo, OH 43624   (419) 255-7055, ext. 221

Charitable Foundations Directory of Ohio, 3rd edition. Ohio Attorney General's Office. 1978. 185 pages. Includes information on 3,500 organizations that report to the Attorney General under state and federal codes: trusts, foundations, charitable organizations. Main section arranged alphabetically by foundation. Indexes by county, purpose, foundation name. $4 prepaid from Charitable Foundations Directory, Attorney General's Office, 30 East Broad Street, 15th Floor, Columbus, OH 43215.

Guide to Charitable Foundations in the Greater Akron Area. Human Services Planning Library. 1978. 63 pages. Based on United Way files, the Attorney General's list and IRS forms 990, as well as information supplied by foundations. Main section lists 42 foundations alphabetically. Sections on scholarship foundations and proposal writing. Appendixes list recently terminated foundations, indexes of assets, grants, subject categories, officers and trustees. $2.50 from Human Services Planning Library, United Way of Summit County, P.O. Box 1260, 90 North Prospect Street, Akron, Ohio.

OKLAHOMA

Oklahoma City Community Foundation
1300 North Broadway
Oklahoma City, OK 73103   (405) 235-5621

Tulsa City-County Library System
400 Civic Center
Tulsa, OK 74103   (918) 581-5144

Directory of Oklahoma Foundations. Thomas E. Broce, editor. 1974. 304 pages. Alphabetical listing of 269 foundations, based on data from cooperating foundations and 1971–72 IRS forms 990. $9.95 from University of Oklahoma Press, 1005 Asp Avenue, Norman, OK 73069.

OREGON

Library Association of Portland
Education and Documents Room
801 S.W. Tenth Avenue
Portland, OR 97205   (503) 223-7201

Directory of Foundations and Charitable Trusts Registered in Oregon. Virgil D. Mills, editor. 1972. Alphabetical listing of 331 foundations, based on 1972 records in Oregon Attorney General's office. $5 prepaid from Department of Justice, 555 State Office Building, 1400 S.W. Fifth Avenue, Portland, OR 97201.

The Guide to Oregon Foundations. Tri-County Community Council, producer. 1977. 263 pages. Based on files at Oregon State Registrar of Charitable Trusts and information from the foundations. Lists 282 alphabetically under five subdivisions: general purpose foundations, special purpose foundations, student aid funds, service clubs and national foundations with an active interest in Oregon. Appendixes list foundations excluded from the guide that have $500,000 in assets or more, or have made grants of $50,000 or more in last fiscal year; regional breakdown, guide personnel, questionnaires, research forms, data on other private funding sources and on national foundations that have made grants in Oregon. $7.50, plus 50 cents postage from Tri-County Community Council, 718 Burnside, Portland, OR 97209.

PENNSYLVANIA

The Free Library of Philadelphia
Logan Square
Philadelphia, PA 19103   (215) 686-5423

Hillman Library
University of Pittsburgh
Pittsburgh, PA 15260   (412) 624-4528

Directory of Pennsylvania Foundations. S. Damon Kletzien, editor, with Margaret H. Chalfant and Frances C. Ritchey. 1978. 304 pages. Alphabetical listings of 1,078 foundations, based on 1975–76 IRS forms 990 and information from the foundations. Appendixes on grant-seeking, indexes of officers, directors and trustees; major interests. $14 prepaid from Friends of the Free Library (Attention: Directory), The Free Library of Philadelphia, Logan Square at Nineteenth Street, Philadelphia, PA 19103.

Pittsburgh Area Foundation Directory. 1976. 97 pages. Lists 194 foundations alphabetically. Based on 1971–74 IRS forms 990. $10 from Community Action Pittsburgh, Inc., Planning and Research Division, Fulton Building, 107 Sixth Street, Pittsburgh, PA 15227.

RHODE ISLAND

Providence Public Library
Reference Department
150 Empire Street
Providence, RI 02903   (401) 521-7722

A Directory of Foundations in the State of Rhode Island, 2nd Edition. John Parker Huber, editor. 1975. 39 pages. Alphabetical listing of 117 foundations, based on 1973 IRS forms 990. Indexes of city or town, interests, assets, grant range (largest to smallest). Published by Eastern Connecticut State College Foundation, Inc. (Out of print; consult library copy.)

SOUTH CAROLINA

South Carolina State Library
Reader Services Department
1500 Senate Street
Columbia, SC 29211   (803) 758-3181

South Carolina Foundation Directory. Anne K. Middleton, editor. 1978. 53 pages. Lists 203 foundations alphabetically. Based on 1975 IRS forms 990. Indexes by cities and fields of interest. 70 cents in postage stamps from Anne K. Middleton, Assistant Reference Librarian, South Carolina State Library, P.O. Box 11469, Columbia, SC 29211.

A Guide to Foundations of the Southeast, Volume II. Jerry C. Davis, editor. 1975. 200 pages. Lists 131 foundations, based on 1973–74 IRS forms 990. Published by Davis-Taylor Associates, Inc. (Out of print; consult library copy.)

TENNESSEE

Resource Center for Non-Profit Agencies, Inc.
502 Gay Street, Suite 201
P.O. Box 1606
Knoxville, TN 37901   (615) 521-6034

Memphis Public Library
1850 Peabody Avenue
Memphis, TN 38104   (901) 528-2957

A Guide to Foundations of the Southeast, Volume I. Jerry C. Davis, editor. 1975. 255 pages. Lists 238 Tennessee foundations, based on 1973–74 IRS forms 990. Index of officers. Published by Davis-Taylor Associates, Inc. (Out of print; consult library copy.)

TEXAS

The Hogg Foundation for Mental Health
The University of Texas at Austin
Austin, TX 78712   (512) 991-6810

Corpus Christi State University Library
6300 Ocean Drive
Corpus Christi, TX 78412   (512) 991-6810

Dallas Public Library
Grants Information Service
1954 Commerce Street
Dallas, TX 75201   (214) 748-9071, ext. 332

EL Paso Community Foundation
El Paso National Bank Building
Suite 1616
El Paso, TX 79901   (915) 533-4020

Houston Public Library
Bibliographic and Information Center
500 McKinney Avenue
Houston, TX 77002   (713) 224-5441, ext. 265

Funding Information Library
Minnie Stevens Piper Foundation
201 North St. Mary's Street, Suite 100
San Antonio, TX 78205   (512) 227-8119

Directory of Texas Foundations, 2nd edition. William J. Hooper, editor. 1978. 184 pages. Lists 1,400 foundations, based on 1971–78 (mostly 1977) IRS forms 990 and 150 telephone calls to key foundations. Indexes of areas of interest and cities. $17 billed, $15.75 prepaid, from Texas Foundation Research Center, P.O. Box 5494, Austin, TX 78763.

The Guide to Texas Foundations. Southern Resource Center. 1975. 104 pages. Based on data from foundations and from 1973–74 records on file with Texas Attorney General. Main section of 214 entries lists foundations by Dallas, Fort Worth, Houston, and "other cities." Lists those with grants greater than $30,000 a year and includes a brief list of those with grants totalling less than $30,000 a year. Index of foundations. $7.50 prepaid from Southern Resource Center, P.O. Box 5993, Dallas, TX 75222.

UTAH

Salt Lake City Public Library
Information and Adult Services
209 East Fifth South
Salt Lake City, UT 84111   (801) 363-5733

VERMONT

State of Vermont Department of Libraries
Reference Services Unit
111 State Street
Montpelier, VT 05602   (802) 828-3261

A Directory of Foundations in the State of Vermont. Denise M. McGovern, editor. 1975. 24 pages. Lists 41 foundations, based on 1972 IRS forms 990. Indexes by city or town, interests, assets, grants. $3 prepaid from Eastern Connecticut State College Foundation, Inc., P.O. Box 431, Willimantic, CT 06226.

VIRGINIA

Grants Resources Library
Ninth Floor, Hampton City Hall
Hampton, VA 23669   (804) 727-6496

Richmond Public Library
Business, Science and Technology Department
101 East Franklin Street
Richmond, VA 23219   (804) 780-8223

Virginia Directory of Private Foundations. Office of Human Resources. 1977. 70 pages. Lists 102 foundations, based on 1974–75 IRS forms 990. Indexes of foundations, geographical areas and religions. $2 prepaid from Department of Intergovernmental Affairs, Fourth Street Office Building, 205 North Fourth Street, Richmond, VA 23219.

WASHINGTON

Seattle Public Library
1000 Fourth Avenue
Seattle, WA 98104   (206) 625-4881

Spokane Public Library
Reference Department
West 906 Main Avenue
Spokane, WA 99201   (509) 838-3361

Charitable Trust Directory. Office of the Attorney General. 1980. 242 pages. Based on 1979 Attorney General's records, lists 968 organizations including charitable trusts that report under the Washington Charitable Trust Act. No indexes. $4 prepaid from Office of the Attorney General, Temple of Justice, Olympia, WA 98504.

WEST VIRGINIA

Kanawha County Public Library
123 Capitol Street
Charleston, WV 25301   (304) 343-4646

West Virginia Foundation Directory. William Seeto, editor. 1979. 49 pages. Lists 99 foundations, based on 1977–78 IRS forms 990. Includes section on inactive or terminated foundations. Index by city and county. $7.95 prepaid from West Virginia Foundation Directory, Box 96, Route 1, Terra Alta, WV 26764.

WISCONSIN

Marquette University Memorial Library
1415 West Wisconsin Avenue
Milwaukee, WI 53233   (414) 224-1515

Foundations in Wisconsin: A Directory, 1978 (3rd edition). Margaret J. Marik, editor. 1978. 337 pages. Lists 645 foundations, based on 1976–77 IRS forms 990. Sections listing inactive foundations, operating foundations, terminated foundations. Indexes of counties, foundation managers, areas of interest in 36 subject categories. $12.50 prepaid (plus 48 cents sales tax or Wisconsin tax-exempt number) from The Foundation Collection, Marquette University Memorial Library, 1415 West Wisconsin Avenue, Milwaukee, WI 53233.

WYOMING

Laramie County Community College Library
1400 East College Drive
Cheyenne, WY 82001   (307) 634-5853

CANADA

The Canadian Centre for Philanthropy
12 Sheppard Street, 3rd Floor
Toronto, Ontario, M5H 3A1   (416) 364-4875

MEXICO

Biblioteca Benjamin Franklin
Londres 16
Mexico City 6, D.F.

PUERTO RICO

Consumer Education and Service Center
Department of Consumer Affairs
Minillas Central Government Building North
Santurce, PR 00904

VIRGIN ISLANDS

College of the Virgin Island Library
St. Thomas
U.S. Virgin Islands 00801   (809) 774-1252

Appendix Two:
For Further Reading

The world of grants

Charity U.S.A.: An Investigation into the Hidden World of the Multi-Billion-Dollar Charity Industry, by Carl Bakal. Times Books, New York, 1979. $16.95. Bakal's big (498 pages) book is an overview of all non-governmental nonprofit funding, and includes excursions into such operations as the Red Cross and the disease charities. But its discussion of fundraising history—4,000 years worth—and its fat second section devoted to donors are worth reading for anyone who wants a general sense of the world of non-profit funding. It's especially telling in its demolition of the myth of corporate generosity.

Foundations Under Fire, edited by Thomas C. Reeves. Cornell University Press, Ithaca and London, 1970. $6.50. This collection of papers and articles describes the attempts at foundation reform a decade ago. Little progress has been made. The best selections are those from the late U.S. Representative Wright Patman of Texas, who preferred to be called a Populist rather than a Democrat, and tried—with only limited success—to make life hell for corporations that diverted money from the Treasury for expenditure on their own political and social purposes.

The Philanthropoids: Foundations and Society, by Ben Whitaker. Morrow,

New York, 1974. $7.95. Whitaker is British, but he was educated at Harvard and has worked in America, and this general survey of foundation giving is probably the most consistently intelligent work in the field. His view of historical trends ends with an examination of those foundations that were willing to front for the CIA, and he is especially witty in his attack on unbridled "grantspeak"—jargon gone amok in the hands of proposal writers.

Philanthropy and the Business Corporation, by Marion R. Fremont-Smith. Russell Sage Foundation, New York, 1972. The Foundation Center has maintained the closest examination of corporate penny-pinching and, as noted in this book, has begun to supply tools for getting at what corporate money there is. This was the pioneering look at how and why corporations give less than the public believes they do and, although almost a decade old, remains accurate in its bleak summary of stinginess on the grand scale.

Why They Give: American Jews and Their Philanthropies, by Milton Goddin. Macmillan, New York, 1976. $10.95. American Jews account for only three percent of the population, but for far more than that percentage of the charity dollar. (In Houston, where I worked for several years, they accounted for less than *two* percent of the population, but for more than twenty-five percent of the charity dollar.) Nor, as this book shows, is their largesse confined to drives for Israel or specifically-Jewish charities. The Jewish cultural attitude toward philanthropy is both a wonder and an example that is explored with warmth and a wealth of anecdote, tracing the great streams of Jewish migration into today's American cities and charities. The key role of Jewish donors is a fundraising commonplace, and here is an excellent way to learn literally everything about it.

Prospect research and grant writing

Many excellent guides in the field are spun off by projects that blink out of existence, taking their publications with them. This is not the case with the State of Oregon or the Taft Organization, each of which generated an excellent but hard-to-find work that concentrates on the proposal itself:

Developing Skills in Proposal Writing, by Mary Jo Hall. Office of Federal Relations, Oregon State System of Higher Education, Corvallis, Oregon, 1977. $10. Oregon, a state noted for its common sense, published this guide to writing proposals for federal research money. It is considered something of a masterpiece in its field, intended to increase Oregon's slice of the federal pie, but available to all those canny enough to find it on library shelves, despite its high ranking on the most-stolen list.

The Proposal Writers Swipe File, edited by Jean Brodsky. Taft Products, Inc., Washington, 1973. Ms. Brodsky and Dick Taft's outfit have supplied the item most novice grant writers want—a fat file of a dozen proposals. Most novice grant writers want them in order to use them as boilerplate, removing the name of the organization as printed and inserting their own. This book defies such folly by eliminating or disguising organizational names and details and by refusing to say exactly how successful the proposals were. Instead of supplying formats for idiots to use, the book shows an amazing diversity of proposal formats and a commitment to good, plain writing—proving just how much competition from the pros the beginner faces. Frightening and inspiring at the same time.

Four general guides, much like the one you are reading now, are usually available in bookstores and libraries. *The Art of Winning Foundation Grants* (1975, $6.95), *The Art of Winning Government Grants* (1977, $7.95) and *The Art of Winning Corporate Grants* (1980, $8.95), aside from providing an education in inflation of book prices, are all by Howard Hillman (and all from Vanguard Press, New York). Hillman is a Harvard Business School graduate with substantial experience in the fundraising field. He preaches a common-sense approach to getting inside the giver's head, which is probably most useful in his book on corporate giving and its long, long list of what turns corporations off (almost anything except projects that fuel positive public relations). The book on government money has a succinct guide to the horrors of the A-95 Clearinghouse process decreed by the Office of Management and Budget to prevent government duplication.

Getting Grants, by Craig W. Smith and Eric W. Skjei, Harper and Row, New York, 1980. Hardbound, $12.95; paperbound, $4.95. Relies on the authors' experience in the field, with many case histories. Its single sample grant proposal, for a youth facility near San Francisco, is well-organized; its chart and discussion comparing the entire nonprofit funding world with the functions of the human heart are hilarious. Especially useful: a 20-page glossary of "grantspeak."

Writing, period.

These are my candidates for the books every grant writer should have on the shelf near his or her typewriter or word processor, all mentioned in the text:

The Art of Readable Writing, by Rudolph Flesch. Harper and Row, New York, 1974 (25th anniversary edition, revised). Dr. Flesch celebrates the genius of plain speaking and plain writing and provides a mathematical system for analyzing the readability and potential impact of your prose. No matter how complicated or arcane your field, you can use his techniques to make your proposal truly readable. Other books *(The Art of Plain Talk, How to Write Plain English)* take his theories further, and the latter volume shows how legalese of all kinds can be translated into useful English.

Elements of Style, by William Strunk, Jr., revised and with additions by E. B. White. Macmillan, New York, 1979. Hardbound, $4.95; paperbound, $1.95. Indispensable.

Harper Dictionary of Contemporary Usage, edited by William and Mary Morris. Harper and Row, New York, 1975. $15. A big panel of writers and editors quarrel brilliantly in this dictionary devoted to troublesome words and constructions. Beautiful because it makes you feel okay about siding with the minority opinion from time to time.

Nuts and bolts

All too few good general guides exist that explain the bookkeeping, accounting, legal and tax problems of nonprofit organizations. One of the big legal publishers, the Commerce Clearing House of Chicago, has provided two works for specialists that contain, buried within them, information you may find handy.

Legal Aspects of Charitable Trusts and Foundations: A Guide for Philanthropoids, by Lois Kutner, Commerce Clearing House, Chicago, 1970, covers all the legal niceties that givers in public and private foundations must answer to.

The Tax Exempt Organization, A Practical Guide, published by the Clearing House in 1969, gathers in one place all of the relevant IRS rules. Look for it in law libraries, or, updated, in law bookstores.

In the tax and accounting fields, the New York law book firm of Matthew Bender has published, since 1973, *Weithorn's Tax Techniques for Foundations and Other Exempt Organizations,* with annual updates.

Readings in Government and Nonprofit Accounting, edited by University of Texas Professor Richard J. Varga. (Wadsworth, Belmont, California, 1977. $6.95.) This very specialized anthology includes papers on an accounting-profession effort to regularize books in the field; your own accountant may find these fascinating.

For the novice grant writer, the old standby *Bookkeeping Made Simple,* by Louis W. Fields, costs only $3.50 as part of Doubleday's eternal "made-simple" series, and does what it claims.

More general information is available in *The Nonprofit Organization Handbook,* by Patricia V. Gaby and Daniel M. Gaby, Prentice-Hall, Englewood Cliffs, N.J., 1978. $35, but worth it.

Appendix Three:
Paperwork

Prospect analysis form

date: _____   page ___ of ___

name _____   address_____

telephone ( ) + _____   _____

Inside Contacts

name	title/function	ext. #

Program Summary	DEADLINES
	apply: _____ internal: _____ file: _____

Grants Analysis

grants to: ___ individuals   ___organizations   ___ shelter institution

grant range: high $_____   low $_____   estimated avg $_____

outside approvals required: _____

maximum % project cost fundable: _____% _____one-time _____sustaining

capital use ok? _____ operations use ok? _____ project-only staff ok? _____

salary limits: _____ institutional overhead ceiling: _____

matching grants: ___makes ___matches/ ratio ___ match deadline _____

special requirements/restrictions: _____

_____

+++

Outside Connections

name	role/task

(See other side for prospect task log.)

Budget

Debt-Counseling Program for Inner City Residents
Buckner, Texas, Urban Resource Center, Inc. 1981.7.1–1982.6.30

	FROM THIS GRANT	IN-HAND, IN-KIND	TOTALS
SALARIES			
1 project director, full-time, @ 22,500/year	22,500		22,500
3 debt counselors (LSWs), half-time @ 16,000/year	10,000	14,900	24,900
1 clerk-receptionist, full-time @ 11,500/year		11,500	11,500
1 publicist, quarter-time @ 18,000/year (URCI staff)		4,500	4,500
	32,500	30,900	63,400
SERVICES			
rent, 6th Street storefront, 1 year @ 5,600/year from (URCI)		5,600	5,600
Municipal Utilities District		1,800	1,800
telephones		800	800
printing, duplicating and other publicity services		5,500	5,500
postage		200	200
travel (state conferences)		600	600
contingencies		2,055	2,055
		15,755	15,755
ONE-TIME START-UP COSTS			
renovations, vacant 6th Street storefront:			
• materials (partitions)		1 100	1,100
• labor (carpenters)	600		600
• materials (glass replacement)		300	300
• labor (glaziers)	150		150
	750	1,400	2,150
	33.250	38,055	71,305

IRS Form 990-AR

Your view of the form on the following pages may change as you play the grants game. At first, it seems to be simply the form that a foundation is obliged, by law, to show to you. As you can see, its tiny blanks provide all-too-little information for the prospect researcher. But if you take the non-profit route of incorporation or association, you may find yourself loath to provide the same information to your rivals. As noted in the text, groups like the National Committee for Responsive Philanthropy would like to see this form expanded tremendously, to give a far more complete picture of income, management, expenditure and motives. This is how it stands now.

Form 990–AR

1979
Annual Report
of Private
Foundation

_____

Name

Under Section 6056 of the Internal Revenue Code

**This Annual Report and
the annual return of the Foundation
filed on Form 990–PF are available for
public inspection. Consult an
Internal Revenue Service office for
further information.**

Annual report for calendar year 1979, or fiscal year beginning _____ , 1979, and ending _____ , 19 _____

Name of organization	Employer identification number

Address of principal office

If books and records are not at above address, specify where they are kept	Name of principal officer of foundation

Public Inspection (See instruction C):

    (a) Enter date the notice of availability of annual report appeared in newspaper ▶ -- .

    (b) Enter name of newspaper ▶---

    (c) Check here ▶ ☐ if you have attached a copy of the newspaper notice as required by instruction C. (If the notice is **not** attached, the report will be considered incomplete.)

Check box for type of annual return ▶ ☐ Form 990–PF ☐ Form 5227 | Check this box if your private foundation status terminated under section 507(b)(1)(A) ▶ ☐

Revenues

1 Amount of gifts, grants, bequests, and contributions received for the year . . . . _____

2 Gross income for the year . . . . _____

3   Total . . . . _____

Disbursements and Expenses

4 Disbursements for the year for exempt (charitable) purposes (including administrative expenses) . . . . _____

5 Expenses attributable to gross income (item 2 above) for the year . . . . _____

Foundation Managers

6 List all managers of the foundation (see section 4946(b)):

Name and title	Address where manager may be contacted during normal business hours

6a List here any managers of the foundation (see section 4946(b)) who have contributed 2 percent of the total contributions received by the foundation before the close of any taxable year (but only if they have contributed more than $5,000). (See section 507(d)(2).)

6b List here any managers of the foundation (see section 4946(b)) who own 10 percent or more of the stock of a corporation (or an equally large portion of the ownership of a partnership or other entity) of which the foundation has a 10 percent or greater interest.

Balance Sheet Per Books at the Beginning of the Year

Assets		Liabilities	
Cash		Accounts payable	
Accounts and notes receivable		Contributions, gifts, grants, etc., payable	
Inventories		Bonds and notes payable	
Securities		Mortgages payable	
Government obligations		Other liabilities	
Corporate bonds		Total liabilities	
Corporate stocks		**Net Worth**	
Mortgage loans		Principal fund	
Real estate . . .			
Less: Depreciation .		Income fund	
Other assets . . .			
Less: Depreciation .		Total net worth	
Total assets		Total liabilities and net worth	

Itemized Statement of Securities and All Other Assets Held at the Close of the Taxable Year

Asset	Book value	Market value
Total . . . . ▶		

Form 990–AR (1979)   Page **4**

Grants and Contributions Paid or Approved for Future Payment During the Year

Recipient Name and address (home or business)	If recipient is an individual, show any relationship to any foundation manager or substantial contributor	Concise statement of purpose of grant or contribution	Amount
Paid during year			
Total . . . . ▶			
Approved for future payment			
Total . . . . ▶			

A notice has been published that this Annual Report is available for public inspection at the principal offices of the foundation, and copies of this Annual Report have been furnished to the Attorney General (or his/her designate) of each State entitled to receive reports as required by instruction F.

▶ --
Signature of foundation manager   Date   ▶ Preparer's signature

▶ --
Title   ▶ Preparer's address

Instructions

A. Annual Report.—An annual report is required from the foundation managers (as defined in section 4946(b)) of every organization which is a private foundation, including a nonexempt trust described in section 4947(a)(1) which is treated as a private foundation, having at least $5,000 of assets at any time during a taxable year. A private foundation may use this form for its annual reporting requirements.

If you prefer not to use this form, you may prepare the report in printed, typewritten or any other form you choose, provided it readily and legibly discloses the information required by section 6056 and the regulations thereunder.

The annual report is in addition to and not in lieu of submitting the information required on Form 990–PF under section 6033.

B. Where and When to File.—

(1) Tax-exempt private foundation.—File the report at the time and place specified for filing Form 990–PF, Return of Private Foundation Exempt from Income Tax.

(2) Nonexempt trust described in section 4947 (a)(1) and treated as a private foundation.—File the report at the time and place specified for filing Form 5227, Return of Nonexempt Charitable or Split-Interest Trust Treated as a Private Foundation under section 4947(a) of the Internal Revenue Code.

C. Public Inspection of Private Foundation's Annual Reports.—As a foundation manager, you must make the annual report required by section 6056 available at the principal office of the foundation for inspection during regular business hours or, if you choose, you may furnish a copy free of charge to such persons requesting inspection, provided these persons do so at the time and manner prescribed in section 6104(d) and the regulations thereunder.

The notice must be published not later than the day prescribed for filing the annual report (including any extensions of time for filing), in a newspaper having general circulation in the county in which the principal office of the private foundation is located. The notice must state that the annual report of the private foundation is available at its principal office during regular business hours for inspection by any citizen who so requests within 180 days after the date of the

publication. It must also show the address of the private foundation's principal office and the name of its principal manager. A private foundation may designate in addition to its principal office, or (if the foundation has no principal office or none other than the residence of a substantial contributor or foundation manager) instead of such office, any other location where its annual report is available.

The term "newspaper having general circulation" will include any newspaper or journal which is permitted to publish statements in satisfaction of State statutory requirements relating to transfer of title to real estate or other similar legal notices.

A copy of the notice must be attached to the annual report filed with the Internal Revenue Service. Because IRS also makes the annual report available for public inspection under section 6104(d), the report and any attachments should be of such quality that they can be reproduced photographically.

A private foundation which has terminated its status as such under section 507(b)(1)(A), by distributing all its net assets to one or more public charities without retaining any right, title or interest in such assets, does not have to publish notice of availability of its annual report or furnish such report to the public for the taxable year in which it so terminates (Reg. 1.507-2(a)(6)). Be sure to check the box on page 2.

D. Signature and Verification.—The report must be signed by the foundation manager.

E. List of States.—A private foundation is required to attach to its Form 990–PF a list of all States:

(1) to which the organization reports in any fashion concerning its organization, assets, or activities, and

(2) with which the organization has registered (or which it has otherwise notified in any manner) that it intends to be, or is a charitable organization or that it is, or intends to be, a holder of property devoted to a charitable purpose.

F. Furnishing of Copies to State Officers; Listing of States.—If the organization has at least $5,000 in assets at any time during the year the foundation managers must furnish a copy of this annual report to the Attorney General (or his/her designate) of (1) each State listed for

Form 990–PF, (2) the State in which the principal office of the foundation is located, and (3) the State in which the foundation was incorporated or organized. The report must be furnished at the same time it is sent to IRS. In addition, the foundation managers must provide upon request a copy of the annual report to the Attorney General or other appropriate State officer of any other State. The foundation managers must also attach to the report a copy of the Form 990–PF (or Form 5227 for a 4947(a)(1) trust) and a copy of the Form 4720 (if any) filed by the foundation with IRS for the year.

G. Penalty for Failure to File Report and Notice on Time.—If a private foundation fails to file the annual report on or before the due date, or to comply with the requirements under instruction C, there will be imposed on the person (anyone under a duty to perform the act) a $10 penalty for each day during which the failure continues, not to exceed $5,000. (See section 6652 (d)(3).)

The penalty of $10.00 a day for failure to file may also be charged if a report is submitted with information omitted. Therefore, please be sure to make an entry in each part of the form even the ones that do not apply to you. If a part or line item does not apply, enter "N/A" (not applicable). (See Rev. Rul. 77–162, 1977–1 C.B. 400, for details.) If more than one person is liable, all such persons will be jointly and severally liable with respect to such failure.

Organizations that have given notice under section 508(b) as to their foundation status and have not received a letter from IRS containing a determination as to such status—refer to Rev. Proc. 79–8, 1979–1 C.B. 487, or later revisions for rules relating to relief from the penalty provision of section 6652. If the failure to file the annual report or comply with instruction C is willful, there will be imposed, in addition to the amount mentioned above, a penalty of $1,000 for each such report or notice. (See section 6685.)

H. Foreign Organizations.—A foreign organization which has received substantially all of its support (other than gross investment income) from sources outside the United States will not be subject to the requirements of instructions C and F above.